L IN A DON'S DAY

Also by Mary Beard

It's a Don's Life
Pompeii: The Life of a Roman Town
The Parthenon
The Colosseum (with Keith Hopkins)
The Roman Triumph

ALL IN A DON'S DAY

Mary Beard

PROFILE BOOKS

First published in Great Britain in 2012 by
PROFILE BOOKS LTD
3A Exmouth House
Pine Street
London EC1R 0JH
www.profilebooks.com

10 9 8 7 6 5 4 3 2 1

Typeset in Minion by MacGuru Ltd
info@macguru.org.uk
Printed and bound by CPI Group (UK) Ltd, Croydon, CR0 4YY

A CIP catalogue record for this book is available from the British Library.

ISBN 978 1 84668 536 1
eISBN 978 1 84765 863 0

Introduction

My blog, 'A Don's Life', has been running for six years now, since early 2006, regularly commenting on a whole range of things that matter to me ... from ancient jokes to A levels, political humbug to Latin mottoes. According to the usual life-expectancy of blogs, six years puts 'the Don' well into late middle age (like its author, in fact). For blogging, as everyone knows, is rather like going to the gym: easy to start, and to work out enthusiastically for a few months, harder to stick at when the novelty has worn off.

Like most regular, long-term gym users, I have kept going for two main reasons: enjoyment and discipline. Enjoyment? Well, after a sceptical start, I soon found that I really relished writing these little essays, composed late at night on the kitchen table. It was fun to point out why that evening's television programme on Roman banquets hadn't got it quite right (p. 15) or to share a discovery I'd made in the library that day (p. 201). And it felt almost therapeutic to reflect on what was really happening day-to-day at the front line of university teaching (none of those long holidays you read about, and precious few claret-swilling dinners, I promise – try the truth about reference-writing, p. 100, or the Human Resources Compliance Unit, p. 140). I loved the immediacy of it all: you think, you write, you click on 'publish' and it's out there.

And discipline? My firm rule has been two posts a week, rain or shine (with only very, very occasionally a third thrown in). The point about blogging – like the exercise routine – is that you have to set your target at something manageable, and never waver. The best advice I could give to a would-be blogger is *don't post every day in your first flush of enthusiasm*; you'll never keep it up.

And after that, the best advice would be to try and attract a community of readers, who will comment on your site thoughtfully, wittily and politely. In general, blog commenters as a species do not have a good name. You don't have to trawl very far in the comment areas of even the most high-minded and liberal blogs, or in the 'Have Your Say' sections of the BBC website or serious broadsheet newspapers, to come across pages and pages of abusive, uninteresting and often deeply sexist responses. ('This is rubbish. Who got you to write this trash? Stick to your knitting, granny' and far worse.) What encourages otherwise perfectly ordinary and polite people to write like this on-line is a mystery to me (though I offer some suggestions on p. 245). But the 'Don's Life' commenters, both the regulars and the occasional visitors, are a very different breed. They may disagree strongly with what I have to say, but they comment with tremendous style, as well as courtesy – contributing intriguingly arcane facts, quirky anecdotes, specially composed verses and multilingual jokes. The distinctive character of 'A Don's Life' comes in part from this (rare) dialogue between poster and commenters.

It is for that reason that this second book of selections from the blog, covering the years 2009–2011, continues the tradition of the first selection (*It's A Don's Life*, 2009) and includes some comments as well as my posts. Both appear almost exactly as they did on-line. I have only occasionally trimmed, corrected the typos, inserted much-needed apostrophes (mine, not the commenters'), ungarbled the garbling and every now and then added a bit of crucial information that was originally delivered through the hyper-links (which are one advantage the web has over the printed page).

Blogs are, in a way, a version of autobiography, or of a diary. And I'm struck, whenever I read my past posts (not a regular habit of mine, you'll be relieved to know), how much, in some respects, my life has changed since I started blogging in 2006. Over the past few years, I have been very lucky indeed. I've been handed some great opportunities and I've done things that twenty years ago (as an exhausted junior lecturer with two small kids and a pretty dismal publication record) I could hardly have dreamt of. No one back then – least of all me – would possibly have predicted that, well past fifty and uncompromisingly grey-haired, I would have ended up presenting television programmes on the Romans on BBC2. (You'll find some of the inside story on these programmes on pp. 173, 178, 226.)

But the changes are only at the margins. The bottom line is that most of my time and energy goes to my day job, as a university teacher and Classicist, and as part-time Classics editor at the *Times Literary Supplement* (where I've worked for almost twenty years now and which is the generous host of my blog). At the *TLS* I commission reviews and then patiently wield an old-fashioned pencil to edit them (inserting all those apostrophes that the commenters complain I so often omit myself). In the university I'm occupied a good twelve hours a day giving lectures, researching in libraries and archives, supervising undergraduates, setting exams, writing articles, marking essays, advising doctoral candidates, attending seminars, visiting schools, ordering library books, responding to government 'targets', assessing theses, interviewing would-be students … and all the other things that come with the territory of being a professional academic. I suspect that some of this work doesn't come over very loud and clear in the blog, and as a consequence my life appears a bit more glamorous than it really is. The reason for that is simple. It's perfectly OK to blog about BAFTAs and filming, or about flying round the world to conferences. It's even occasionally OK to sound off about the university's HR department. It really isn't fair to share with the world your day-to-day frustrations at a student's lousy essay, at the silly things some unfortunate candidate said in an interview or for that matter at the incomprehensible last paragraph cobbled together by an inexperienced reviewer. But those things are my bread and butter.

The university that has employed me for most of my working life is the University of Cambridge (and I am a fellow of Newnham College, still – I'm glad to say – for women only). As I hope 'A Don's Life' does capture, Cambridge is a wonderful and in many ways a privileged place to work, and it has some quirks and customs, both charming and irritating, that you will not find in any other university anywhere, except perhaps Oxford. For good or ill, there are only a handful of educational institutions worldwide where the wording of a Latin grace could possibly a cause of controversy between students and teachers (p. 32). But Cambridge is also a much more ordinary university than newspapers, television and movies like to suggest. It has cash shortages, cuts, early retirements, new-style management rules and jargon, risk assessments, impoverished students, compliance units and exhausted staff – just like any other. The vast majority of us – students or teachers – don't live the 'Cambridge myth'; we don't punt or drink port or wear blazers. And we haven't come from dynasties of Oxbridge graduates (for what it's worth, I am the first member of my family to get a university degree, Oxbridge or not).

But if you're smart, you won't study or teach in Cambridge for long without finding a way of *coming to terms* with the myth – knocking it on the head (p. 91), parodying it or, best of all, somehow find a way of turning it to your own advantage. And that's exactly what we find the intrepid investigative journalists of the student newspaper doing in the first post in this selection, when (tongue in cheek) they decide to do a survey on how rich the Mummies and Daddies of Cambridge undergraduates really are, and which the poshest colleges might be …

How rich are Cambridge students?

29 January 2009

One of the local student newspapers – *Varsity* – has got another scoop. Last term it conducted an online questionnaire, which apparently revealed that 50% of Cambridge students had at some time or other in their university career 'plagiarised' (whatever that meant).

I wasn't sure how much weight to put on these anonymous confessions, honestly. But now *Varsity* has run a new questionnaire to find out how rich the average Cambridge student is and how much their parents earn – and, for the benefit of the punters, they've broken this down by college and Tripos subject. It's the lead story this week, even upstaging the article on that burning Cambridge controversy on the wine served to students at St John's Formal Hall. (That's irony, by the way, before you write in …)

Some of this new scoop plays to our usual prejudices. History of Art comes out top of the subject 'rich list' – with a claimed average weekly budget per student of £182 per week and an average parental income of £118k. Not enough to buy young Rupert a Caravaggio to work on, but still a generous cushion against poverty.

But there were other, surprising, results.

I'm not sure whether to believe the stories of students who claim to have to feed themselves by scavenging from supermarket bins or, for that matter, the stories of those who claim to drink bars dry of champagne. They are both boasts, of a different variety, I half-suspect. Of course, if they're

true, I have hugely more sympathy with the former than the latter, but (rather primly) would advise both to go and talk to their college's financial tutor. Most colleges have funds to help students who are really short of money, and they also understand the problem of student debt – which certainly is

getting worse. They no doubt have plenty of advice to dispense
to the stupidly spendthrift too.

But it was funny to see the average parental income at
King's (with all its radical image) coming out well above St
John's (with all their wine at Formal Hall problems). And
what about the women of Murray Edwards College – which
is still 'New Hall' to most of us, partly because its new name
sounds more like a rugby prop than a college – having Mums
and/or Dads bringing in £108k and at the top of the college
table? Old-fashioned Peterhouse, with all its slight *hauteur*,
had an average family income of £54,800, putting it at the very
bottom (and reassuringly at first sight for those who want to
dispel Cambridge's snobby image), rather lower than twice the
median wage of a forty- to forty-nine-year-old in the UK.

It was at this point that I began to see the problem with this
bit of online 'research'. It wasn't just that there were only 783
respondents (fewer than 40 per college). That's not a bad rate
as Cambridge student questionnaires go, actually. And it's not
that they were all lying.

Isn't the problem that most of these students don't have
the foggiest clue what their parents take home? And isn't
it possibly the rich who are least aware of what the family
income is and where it comes from? After all, they're not
always having to fill in benefit and claim forms with exactly
that kind of information.

Still a nice try, *Varsity*!

Dixon of Dock Green on-line

25 February 2009

A few weeks ago we registered for 'e-cops'. This is Cambridge's attempt to keep the police in touch with the local community by sending out email news of crime in your area and what the boys in blue are doing to apprehend the offenders.

I had been rather looking forward to this. But for the first few weeks it was deeply disappointing. Was there so little crime in leafy Cambridge that all they could put in the emails were invitations to crime education events? Or were they keeping something from us?

'Once more we will be celebrating Valentine's Day – helping people in need of some crime prevention', ran the e-bulletin on 28 January (urging us to come and find out about more about window locks). This was quickly followed up by a message suggesting that we might like to put an 'In Case of Emergency' (ICE) number on the contacts of our mobile phones.

Nanny state stuff.

But recently things have looked up. Particularly exciting was the Sergeant's blog that arrived on 11 Feb.

Paul (for that is the Sergeant's name) explained to his flock that he'd been a bit too busy for blogging recently, working on two ASBO applications. But he was now back on-line. There had been, he went on, an upturn in 'dwelling burglaries', but the good news was that two felons had been 'recalled' to prison. And this was followed by a tally of road traffic penalties in our area: 38 penalties for no seat belt worn; 27 penalty notices for using a mobile phone; 7 vehicle rectification defect scheme notices; 5 speeding tickets; 1 penalty notice for using a bus lane etc. etc. (It wasn't clear what the period for this was: a week? a month? a day?) Finally came the report of 'four "days of action" at the Fen Drayton Nature Reserve to tackle mini moto and off road vehicle nuisance'. ('As is a Sergeant's lot I sat on the side lines whilst Phil and Dave had their fun in the two BMXF650 off road bikes …')

In less than two weeks, there was another blog. This time Sergeant Paul had been doing 'a bit of hiding behind walls' in the Histon area and (oh dear) had 'had a productive hour' in the village centre 'finding four people with cannabis'. *(Four people with cannabis wandering round sleepy Histon, in a single hour … ??)* Then there was more good news about burglary arrests, some intelligence about possibly rogue cold callers in Swavesey – and a mysterious 'potentially volatile community situation within Cambridge City', which had got the Sergeant up early in the morning ('resolved …. very quietly').

At first, I confess, I had rather chuckled at all this. It was all too like Dixon to be true. But then I kicked myself for my snooty lack of generosity. Because, actually, Sergeant Paul's commitment to the job came across loud and clear. He is obviously a decent chap who (apart from those four poor cannabis users, and the unfortunate ASBO victims) is doing a great job. And, yes, if I had a burglary I'd be happy to see him knocking at my front door.

Which I guess is the point of e-cops.

Comments

Last week, our e-cops summary contained a number of hidden gems, but 'As well as above please remember to register your electrical goods or anything with a cereal number' was the line that had us in fits of laughter for some time …
CRIS

For us not in the loop, please explain 'ASBO'
PL

It's an Anti-Social Behaviour Order, which (to cut a long story short) can curtail the movement etc. of those who have 'indulged' in anti-social behaviour.

Opinions differ as to whether they: a) protect innocent grannies from having their gardens wrecked by young thugs; or b) provide a counter-productive badge of pride for said thugs/ pick on the relatively innocent/shift the anti-social behaviour elsewhere not eradicate it.
MARY BEARD

Transparency is the new opacity

11 March 2009

I have spent the evening writing my 'supervision reports' –
termly assessments for the students I'm teaching for essay
work, either in small groups or 'one to one'. There's a strong
incentive to get them done on time, because you don't get paid
until you've submitted them. (OK, I know that at most other
universities people don't get paid extra for this kind of work …
In defence I'd say that teachers at Oxford and Cambridge have
traditionally had more 'contact hours' of this sort than those at
other universities.)

In the old days you used to do these on little sheaves of
carbon paper, which made several copies of each of your
reports (one for you, one for the director of studies, one for
the tutor etc.). You sent these off in the mail, and the director
of studies would mediate the contents to the students. It was
a good way of reporting on the student's progress, as well as
sharing concerns. 'She never talks when she is in a group with
Jenny.' 'Hasn't she got terribly thin … ?' You relied on the
discretion of the director of studies not to read that kind of
thing out to the student. Occasionally some idiots did. But by
and large the system, and the judgement calls, worked pretty
well. The student got to know how they were doing, and you
could pass on other useful, frank – even if unrepeatable –
comments without fearing that it would be fed direct to the
student concerned.

Now it's all computerised. This has done away with the
infuriating mountain of paper. It also gives the students

direct access to what you have written. No more confidential warnings. It's all bland 'record of achievement' kind of stuff. ('Jenny has made good progress this term. She seems to be mastering making more complex arguments – this was very clear in her essay on the reforms of Tiberius Gracchus' …. and so on.)

OK, this all comes up to new standards of transparency. There are no secret comments hidden from the student. That must be good, mustn't it?

Well yes, except that there's less honesty in the record. All those frank, confidential comments are still made, but 'underground' as it were, and not in the reports. If you have anxieties about, for example, a student's weight loss, or binge-drinking, the temptation is to convey it in a quiet word in the pub, or on the phone. So it never gets written down at all.

This is particularly awkward with graduate students, who get the same kind of open reports. Imagine this fictional scenario. (Don't worry my grads – it really is *fictional* and not about you.)

Suppose that I am supervising a relatively weak PhD student … let's call him Jim. Jim is reaching the end of his fourth year of research and is struggling to finish his thesis, is on the verge of depression and of giving up. (The end of a PhD is a tense time for even the most robust individuals.) Frankly I am not confident that Jim will make it, but I meet him every week, with a pretty upbeat message: what he's written so far is more or less fine, and all he needs to do is get those last 20,000 words done. This isn't entirely true, but if at this point I tell him that his first two chapters aren't really up to scratch and will need a lot more work, he *will* simply give up … and I reckon that the best chance of successful completion is to get some kind of draft finished. Then we can work on improvements. 'Do you really think it's OK?' asks Jim. 'Yes' I say with some caveats ... though Jim doesn't spot the caveats. And I don't really intend him to.

Then the termly report has to be filled in on-line. The truth I ought to be conveying is that we have a potential disaster on our hands here, but if Jim reads that, he'll simply give up or go right over the edge. It'll be a self-fulfilling prophecy, and he'll accuse me of gross hypocrisy to boot. So I tailor something to be not entirely untrue, but with roughly the same upbeat message that I'm transmitting weekly and not much anxiety showing. ('Although there has been some slippage in his timetable, Jim is now making great strides towards completion ...')

Let's suppose I don't win with Jim, and he does give up – or finishes but doesn't pass. My colleagues try to find out what went wrong and summon up all the reports. There's not a single one which predicts the disaster that came. The disaster was completely unpredictable, they conclude.

No it wasn't, I think. This isn't transparency, it's opacity in a new guise. Can't we accept that a bit of secrecy might be a price worth paying for honesty?

Comments

Yeah, Jim's a worry ... but what is the actual difficulty here? Wasn't it better he should give up, which Mary put all that effort into coaxing him not to do?

PAUL

Wouldn't it be possible to try and be frank with this fictional Jim well before it comes to potential disaster? If he doesn't think you've noticed and you continue giving him positive feedback, he won't ask for help he knows he needs or for the push he knows he should get (let's face it, sometimes you know you need a good solid push from your supervisor).

ZAREEN

The laughter lover

15 March 2009

I should have known that giving a big lecture about the late Roman joke book (called the *The Laughter Lover* or, in Greek, *Philogelos)* in Comic Relief week would attract more interest in this particular byway of the Classics than usual. But when – months ago – I fixed the date to go to Newcastle for the gig, I hadn't realised that it *was* Comic Relief.

In fact, I didn't actually realise the coincidence till someone pointed it out just before the lecture started. 'Funny you're lecturing on Roman jokes when it's Red Nose Day tomorrow,' they said.

Anyway, thanks to the efficient press release put out by Newcastle University, there had already been a number of media inquiries to my mobile phone before I reached the banks of the Tyne. In this case, they were quite hard to deal with. The problem was that most of the journalists had got the impression that I had actually discovered – or dug up, perhaps – a new and entirely unknown book of Roman jokes.

The *Daily Mail* asked if they could have a picture of it and didn't seem quite to think that a picture of Roger Dawe's published edition in the Teubner text series (which is all I could offer) was actually what they were looking for.

It was hard to get the point across that the text had been known for centuries (Dr Johnson had been keen on it, and Jim Bowen had recently performed parts of it), but that I was looking at it harder than anyone had done for ages and in a new way. That's what being 'new' is, for the most part, in Classics.

Still, I soon found that having a little repertoire of ancient jokes that I could quote, tailored to the paper or show in question, did the trick. I even found some that pleased the man from *The Sun*

I think the biggest hit with *The Sun* was this one.

'A man says to his sex-crazed wife, 'What shall we do tonight – have dinner or have sex?' 'Whichever you like,' she replied, 'but there's no bread.'

Oddly the interest didn't fade once Red Nose Day had passed. The *Today* programme wanted a joke or two for the programme on Saturday morning. This was a bit of a problem, as I was due at my Speed Awareness Training in Milton Keynes by 9.30 (and the husband had rightly said that I was to be out of the house by 7.30). In the end, I told the gags over the phone at 7.25, before zooming (no, not zooming) off in the car.

But not before the World Service had rung to ask for an interview for *Newshour*. The only time for this was in the car park at the Safety Training Centre, *if* I got there in good time.

I did, and spent the last few minutes before 9.30 pre-recording an interview via my mobile, to be used later in the day. Plaudits where they are due. The World Service outstripped even the *Today* programme in intelligence. There was no need to explain the nature of the 'discovery', and we spent five minutes talking about the interesting way that these Roman jokes played on questions of disputed identity (which I'm particularly interested in).

And I gave them my favourite joke.

'Three men – a *scholasticos* (an egghead), a barber and a bald man – were going on a long journey and had to camp out at night. They decided to take it in shifts to watch over the luggage. The barber took the first shift, but got bored. So to pass the time, he shaved the head of the *scholasticos* – then woke him up to take his turn. The *scholasticos* got up, rubbed his head and found that he had no hair. 'What an idiot that barber is,' he said, 'he's woken up baldy instead of me.'

Comments

Commenters couldn't resist adding some more favourite scholasticos *(or* scholastikos*) jokes from* The Laughter Lover ...

My favourite *scholasticos* joke is the one in which the *scholasticos* hears that one of a pair of identical twin brothers has died. When he meets the surviving brother, he asks, 'So who died, you or your brother?'

GILBERT L. GIGLIOTTI

I like this one, which seems to me quite subtle. A *scholastikos*, having dreamt he had stepped on a nail, is bandaging his foot. His fellow *scholastikos* asks why and, on learning the reason, says 'No wonder they call us stupid! Why ever do you sleep barefoot?'

MICHAEL BULLEY

... before moving on to the press ...

Many of the sensational headlines are promoted by universities' press offices. Sometimes I feel sorry for the press officers because it requires a good imagination and cross-cultural thinking to sell ideas in this way. My own esteemed seat of learning once regaled the papers with stories of how its evolutionary psychology bods had discovered that mammals with bigger brains had a better chance of escaping predators. I saluted the free rag *Metro* when the latter reported this story ironically under the headline 'No shit Sherlock!'

SW FOSKA

Heston's Roman feast

25 March 2009

Heston Blumenthal's historic cookery series on Channel 4 took on Roman food this week (filmed, I guess, before his Fat Duck restaurant had its nasty brush with the norovirus). There was plenty of luxury and sex (almost) on display. The Romans, we learned, were 'theatrical, deviant and orgasmic' – and Heston set out to recreate their theatrical, deviant and orgasmic food for a group of celebs who had been hired to consume and comment on the finished product.

There was a lot of library work going on in the background, and plenty of pictures of Heston scanning the Loeb edition of Petronius' *Satyricon*. But the fun came in seeing if he could actually make the dishes.

He did rather well with the Roman staple of *garum* – their favourite sauce, made out of rotten fish, which, as Heston pointed out, they seem to have smeared over most things. It is this that usually defeats undergraduate Roman dinner parties (anchovy paste doesn't quite get it). But even if Heston didn't have the patience to rot his fish for the three months that the Romans did, he did manage to heat up and blend together a load of mackerel intestines, so that they ended up looking rather like a Thai sauce which was (so Heston insisted) really 'delicious'.

The most interesting bit for me was the recreation of the 'Trojan pig'. This is a joking dish described by Petronius in the *Satyricon*, but known elsewhere in Roman literature. It's a large roast pig stuffed with sausages, so that when the flesh of the pig is slit, what looks like intestines tumble out.

In Petronius, it is a neat joke played on the dinner guests, staged between the host, Trimalchio, and his cook. The pig is brought in to the banquet, and with it comes the cook – full of apologies that he has forgotten to gut the animal. Trimalchio feigns anger and orders the cook to strip for a whipping, until the other guests plead for mercy. 'OK,' says Trimalchio, 'gut it now.' And out come all those sausages ... and everyone applauds.

Heston had rather more trouble with this one.

He ended up having to push the pig in on a great trolley and arrange it rather awkwardly to have its belly slit. The sausages had been very carefully positioned inside, using a medical endoscope to get them in just the right place (not a facility available in the Roman kitchen). Even so, when the knife went in, nothing exactly tumbled out very impressively ... even though the celebs made suitable 'ooh aah' noises, and he eventually managed to present them with a trayful of what you might easily have mistaken for innards.

He had better luck with Petronius' ejaculating cake, which was the centrepiece of his Roman pudding.

So how did Heston score for authenticity? Could have been worse, I thought. True, it was the same old stuff about the Romans being the world's first bulimics, and I kept having a nasty feeling that we were going to be told that old myth about them vomiting between courses (though we never actually were). And there wasn't even a gesture to the fact that, even if the rich really did eat this sort of stuff (which they probably didn't – the *Satyricon* is a fantasy novel, for heaven's sake), the poor were on a much more subdued diet of cheese, fruit and cabbage.

All the same, I'm pleased to report that he passed what I once called the 'dormouse test'. ('The longer you have to wait for a dormouse to appear in a recreated Roman banquet, the more accurate the reconstruction is likely to be.') We learned about the Romans eating flamingos and sows' udders, and there was a lurid sequence in which Heston whipped up a calf's brain custard. But there was not a dormouse in sight.

Comments

I too was wondering when we going to get to the dormouse. I suspect that the procedure used for fattening the poor creatures didn't make it past the welfare people – though to judge by Heston's demeanour in the slaughterhouse, or when cheerfully disembowelling live fish, he wouldn't have minded.

The last dish, the 'ejaculating cake', seemed to have been made largely of chocolate. Not too many points for authenticity there, methinks.

NELSON JONES

Should schools teach Twittering?

3 April 2009

There was much hand-wringing a few days ago about the idea that primary schools should give up teaching kids about the nineteenth century and should teach them about blogs, Twittering and Wiki instead.

The thing that bothered me most about this was not the elevation of Twittering skills above (say) poetry, but the idea that central government would be requiring Twittering (or whatever) of all schools in England. More imposition of a one-size-fits-all model on to long-suffering, and very diverse, teachers and pupils.

I can't see anything wrong, in itself, in teaching kids about all kinds of different uses of languages and styles and genres. In fact, I vividly remember when I was about twelve, being required to practise writing telegrams in an English lesson at school. (And telegrams were almost the 1960s' equivalent of Twitter, weren't they?)

The task set, I still recall, was to write a telegram to someone who had won a scholarship to Cambridge and ask them to confirm that they would be taking it up (an exercise that was also presumably one of the drip, drip ways in which our academic aspirations were raised.) My own effort (of which I'm even now quite proud) was: 'WON SCHOLARSHIP CAMBRIDGE WIRE IF ACCEPTING'. (I thought it was clear enough without 'STOP' between 'CAMBRIDGE' and 'WIRE'.)

Not a bad exercise in concision. And nor would Twittering be, I suspect.

As it happens, you will be pleased, surprised or utterly horrified to learn that 'A Don's Life' itself has already featured in one area of the nation's pedagogy. One of my friends has just published a book (*World and Time: Teaching Literature in Context*) which, among other things, aims to help teachers with ways of teaching literary analysis in all kinds of different genres. There's all sorts of stuff in it: Wordsworth, Eliot, Zadie Smith, Virginia Woolf, Julian Barnes and … well … of all the unlikely things … me. To be precise, there's an old blog posting called 'Self-promotion?' It was written when my book *The Roman Triumph* came out and talked about publicity drives ('I started the week with *Start the Week*. It gets 2 million listeners, so is probably the biggest audience who'll ever get to hear about the book') and launch parties ('one in a really great location in Greek St – perfect place to have a *Triumph* party … geddit?'). And it went on to fess up to the terror and anticipation of the first reviews. 'So far I've done pretty well, and luckily. There was a great piece in the *Sunday Times* … But don't worry it hasn't gone to my head! Partly because of the little torrent of bile poured over me by Freddy Raphael in the *Spectator*.'

The other writers collected in *World and Time* (those that are still with us, that is) may be well used to people dissecting their poetry and prose, but I have never seen anyone having a go at mine before. I expected to think that they had got it all wrong, or that they pointed to clever little stylistic features that were entirely unintentional. But not a bit of it. The book put its finger instantly on the chummy yet crafted familiar tone of the blog (the 'geddit' and the '*Freddy* Raphael'), the insistent addresses direct to the reader ('Don't worry') and the (trying hard to be) casual repetitions ('I started the week with *Start the Week*'). It also rightly picked me up on some inelegant repetitions of the not very pretty word 'pretty'.

And at the end of the section there were some topics and questions to be tried on the pupils: 'Can a blog really claim to be taken seriously as a literary text?' or 'Do we read blogs on-screen differently from the way we read essays on a page?'

I think I'm really quite happy at a few kids dipping into my blog and wondering about writing and literature in the electronic age. (Well, I would be quite happy, wouldn't I?) But the idea that the whole of the school population should be *forced* to hone their literary skills on 'A Don's Life' – even I think that's a nightmare vision of pedagogy.

Comments

Businesses used to be telegraphic addresses, in order to save telegram senders money on words. Blackwell's was BOOKS OXFORD (which seemed a little hard on its neighbour, which was simply BODOX). The Oxford Union Society was ACME OXFORD – one sometimes wondered if the M was a misprint for an N. The notes that come with a passport (sometimes the only thing to read on a Turkish bus journey) recorded that the telegraphic address of all British consulates was BRITAIN followed by the name of the city and of High Commissions was UKREP followed by the name of the city, which made sense. More mysterious was the information that the telegraphic address of all British embassies was PRODROME followed by the name of the city – what had Her Britannic Majesty to do with St John the Baptist?

OLIVER NICHOLSON

The on-line dictionary of protocol gives this definition of
PRODROME and its use in British telegraphy:

PRODROME. The telegraphic address of the Foreign and
Commonwealth Office, first registered in 1884. Taken from the
Greek *prodromos* meaning 'precursor', it was probably chosen on
the assumption that most telegrams were precursors of longer
and more informative despatches. In 1911, following the Italian
invasion of the Ottoman province of Tripoli, it was allegedly
mistaken by the Italian military censors for the address of a press
agency, and the telegrams of the British consul-general, who was
considered unfriendly, were blocked.

TONY FRANCIS

The history girls vs. David Starkey

David Starkey (whom I have criticised before for being a trifle inaccurate on the history of the ancient world) has been sounding off in the *Radio Times* about how 'feminised' history has become: not a development of which he is in favour.

He's talking about his new TV series on Henry VIII: 'One of the great problems has been that Henry, in a sense, has been absorbed by his wives. Which is bizarre. But it's what you expect from feminised history, the fact that so many of the writers who write about this are women and so much of their audience is a female audience. Unhappy marriages are big box office.'

If only it were true, I found myself thinking. Much as I admire the work of my male colleagues in ancient history, I think that the subject could only be improved by being a bit more 'feminised'. And, so far as I can see from my Cambridge vantage point, there's not much sign of modern British history in universities being a bastion of women's power and influence. In fact, it's usually said of the gender balance in UK history departments that the further from the 'central periods' of British history a subject is, the more likely you'll find a woman teaching it. We're let in at the margins, in other words.

But what does a feminised history mean anyway? Is it history for women, by women, about women?

Predictably enough, the papers have collected outraged responses from women who have written about women: Amanda Foreman, author of *Georgiana, Duchess of Devonshire*,

Lisa Hilton, author of *Athenais, The Real Queen of France*, and many others. These are excellent historians in their way, I'm sure. But the point of 'feminising' history isn't just to pretend that women were as powerful or as influential as men, and then to write about them in the same old fashion.

The *Sunday Times*, enjoying a dig at Starkey, cited some of the famous women who had been powerful in the history of the Roman world, and who shouldn't get left out of the story: Messalina (the adulterous wife of the emperor Claudius) and Agrippina (her successor and the mother of Nero); Cleopatra and the emperor Constantine's mother, Helena.

But hang on, I thought, isn't it a bit more complicated? Surely we have hardly any clue at all about whether Messalina or Agrippina really were powerful; what we know is that they were useful symbols on to which Roman writers themselves projected all the ills of their political system. I'm not saying that they were demure, shrinking violets. But they were certainly convenient targets for ridicule and abuse, useful figures to blame for a whole range of disasters that afflicted the Roman imperial house. Someone's just died ... must have been poisoned by Agrippina! A history book based around Agrippina makes even less sense (and must be even more speculative) than one based around the emperor Nero.

I thought feminising history was about doing history differently, and having different assumptions about what power was. The sort of history, for example, that doesn't always start from the antics of ye olde royal family, and Tudors in tights, perhaps?

Comments

Wow. What exactly is the problem? And how exactly does history
become 'feminised'? By finally paying attention to women in
history, perhaps? I for one am just becoming aware of the vast
corpus of convent chronicles from the late medieval period and
early Renaissance, and it's quite clear that, once a large number
of them are finally translated, they will be seen as an actual *genre*
in the hulking shadow of humanist literature. By women, about
women and for women. Bring it on, I say!

JOHN T

Isn't most of the written evidence about Agrippina (both of
them), Messalina and Cleopatra the work of elite males with the
benefit of 'hindsight'? And almost entirely hostile. If you look
at the contemporary evidence, coins, statues etc., the picture
is completely different. Agrippina, for example, is seen as a
conduit, linking the past with the future, a sister, wife and mother
of emperors. Power may have been a step too far for most, but
women have always had influence. It's about time male historians
recognised the fact.

JACKIE

Norman Mailer once said of feminism in academia: Down with
bulls–t, up with cows–t! And it can be, too.

MARION DIAMOND

Pirates? Try the Pompey-the-Great solution?

13 April 2009

Piracy, it seems, has always been with us, and still is. Or, at least, as we've seen this last week with the piracy off the Somali coast, there are still people we don't like doing nasty things on the high seas with tragic consequences.

Exactly who is to count as a 'pirate' as such will always remain a matter of opinion and dispute. For 'pirates' are no more objectively defined than 'terrorists'. To most of the world, after all, Sir Francis Drake was a dreadful pirate; to the British he still somehow manages to qualify as an 'explorer'.

But however you define them, the Romans had plenty of trouble with criminals sailing around the Mediterranean. It must sometimes have seemed hard to decide which was the greater danger of a sea voyage in antiquity: shipwreck or kidnapping by one of the many gangs of thugs looking to make quick money by getting ransoms for the wealthy individuals they captured (or alternatively by selling them into slavery).

The most famous victim of this was the young Julius Caesar, who fell into pirate hands in the 70s BC. The story of this crime was almost certainly later embellished to make it a nice prequel of Caesar's later character and career. It is said that when the pirates told him that they were going to demand 20 talents ransom money (a hefty sum), Caesar replied that he was worth much more than that – and insisted that they double it.

Some of his party went off to get the cash, leaving Caesar to live for a month or so with his captors. He is supposed to have treated them as servants, telling them not to make too much noise when he wanted to rest, making them listen to him practising his oratory and threatening that when he was released he would have them crucified. When the ransom arrived, he was set free – and indeed, in due course, he did crucify the lot of them.

But it was Caesar's great rival Pompey the Great (pictured above) who had greatest success against the pirates, with a rather more liberal approach.

By the early 60s BC, pirates had become such a menace to Mediterranean shipping that in 67 Rome gave Pompey a 'special command' and vast resources to try to get rid of them. It was a great opportunity for this general 'on the make' to demonstrate his military genius. So he divided the sea into separate operational regions and, using loyal subordinate officers, he swept the pirates off the waters in just a few months.

But Pompey was smart enough to realise that, unless they were given some other form of livelihood, they would soon be back. (This is basically the Afghanistan problem: if they don't make their money out of the poppy crop, how *are* they going to survive.) So in a wonderful, early 'resettlement of offenders' initiative he offered the pirates smallholdings near the coast, where they could make an honest living for themselves.

In fact, Servius, the late Roman commentator on the works of Virgil, was convinced that his poet had given one of these reformed characters a walk-on part in the *Georgics* (4, 125ff.): an old man, living near Tarentum in south Italy, peacefully keeping bees, his days of piracy long behind him.

Might this not be a better solution than a shoot-out for the Somali pirates?

Comments

One of the most riveting lectures I ever heard was a description by J. N. L. Myres (former Bodley's Librarian and Anglo Saxonist) of how his father, J. L. Myres, (*Who were the Greeks?*) spent a large part of the Great War cattle-rustling on the western littoral of Asia Minor, thereby tying down large numbers of Turkish forces who might otherwise have been employed at Gallipoli or Kut or against Allenby. I seem to recall that his privateering activities came to an end when he rustled some cattle belonging to the family of the Greek wife of W. R. Paton (*Loeb Greek Anthology*). I suspect that the pamphlet which resulted from the lecture, 'The Blackbeard of the Aegean: Commander J. L. Myres R.N.V.R.', is now something of a rare bibliographical item.

OLIVER NICHOLSON

Literary ladies at Cambridge – and who's minding the baby?

27 April 2009

There are many nice things about being a fellow of Newnham College. I could go on at great length about the virtues even (or especially) in 2009 of having a college for women only. But I will spare you, till later. This weekend I've been thinking instead about Newnham's literary inheritance. Among our alums (as I have now almost got used to calling them) is a range of the best, and best-known, writers of the twentieth century: A. S. Byatt, Margaret Drabble, Claire Tomalin, Sylvia Plath, Joan Bakewell, Germaine Greer, Katharine Whitehorn, Sarah Dunant – and many more.

So it was partly in celebration of this that the Cambridge Wordfest (the local literary festival) held some appropriate events in Newnham this year, and the college hosted a dinner for the speakers and assorted others, me included. Almost all of us had some connection with Newnham; most had been students or on the staff at one time or another.

There were fourteen of us 'girls', and those at my end of the table included Frances Spalding and Isabelle Grey (who was in my year in Newnham when I was an undergraduate), plus Jean Wilson. And after dinner I quaffed – I confess – a lot more claret with Isabelle and Rebecca Abrams, and the college Vice-Principal, Catherine Seville.

So how was the conversation?

Well, over dinner I talked to Frances about work. She
was about to do a Wordfest session with Susan Sellers on
Virginia Woolf (featuring the very table around which Woolf
famously dined at King's – as she explains in *Room of One's
Own* – an iconic piece of feminist furniture recently loaned to
Newnham), and she has a book on John and Myfanwy Piper
coming out.

But after dinner we fell increasingly to talk, as women do,
about a *woman's lot*. Why is it, when everything should be
swimming for women, that there is still such a gap between
men's and women's lives and careers?

A lot of that, we agreed, is about the 'conceptual economy'
of domestic responsibility. I sit down at lunch with the mothers
who work at Newnham and know that, whatever else they have
been doing (from splitting atoms to lecturing on the Anglo-
Saxons), they have never left their home life entirely behind.
Their heads still must have space for the lost ballet shoes, the
nursery Christmas party and the up-coming vaccinations.

Most men, I am convinced, however much they share
the domestic chores when they are at home, leave them all
behind as soon as they shut the front door. I watch Cambridge
academics at seminars in the early evening. Suppose the
discussion is going really well. You see them calculating if they
can stay later than they should – and quite how apologetic they
are going to have to be when they roll up home an hour late.
Will flowers be enough to compensate? Or a bottle of wine, or
a dinner out? The women don't have a choice; they just leave.

We finished the evening with a tragic *reductio ad absurdum*
of just that point. Isabelle remembered the story of a guy in
America who went to work and simply forgot that he had the
baby in the back of the car, to drop off at daycare. At the end

of the day the baby was found dead, locked in a very hot car in the parking lot.

An urban myth? No, it really happened. And it gives new depths to the old joke: 'Oh my God, I left the baby on the bus.'

Comments

An average of 38 babies died every year between 1998 and 2008 in the US caused by hyperthermia in cars. It seems related to mandatory airbags – this made it illegal to put a small child in the front seat. Babies were put in the back of the car. Out of sight, out of mind.

TONY FRANCIS

Re: 'Most men, I am convinced, however much they share the domestic chores when they are at home, leave them all behind as soon as they shut the front door.'

The 'most' in that sentence might save you here, Mary, since I couldn't produce statistics either. But I'm afraid I don't share your impression. In fact, I'd much prefer that there wasn't this assumption that this is fine/usual/just how men are; it makes it rather difficult for those of us who, however much we like a good academic discussion, also would rather *like* to spend some time at home with the family in the evening.

JIW

Provocative stuff Mary! Our learned friend JIW has beaten me to the punch, but I share his sentiment entirely ... Perhaps the ladies at Newnham might like to invite the likes of James and me to such a discussion. I fancy our rapid exits from meetings/seminars and the like to do the Brownie & Cub run (it's Monday, so that's my task for this evening … Beavers tomorrow, dancing on Wednesday and preparation of 'family meal' on Thursday) are far from unusual in 30-something fathers today.

CHRIS

Even though women consistently get better academic results than the embollocked, the expectations on them are still belittling and destructive. Men are considered attractive on the basis of status, wealth and the possession of corresponding material goods – houses, cars, trophy women/mistresses etc. Women on the basis of their allure re such men. Poor bitches. So go Boudica and slaughter the myriads of jumped-up male parasites and swollen boils currently infesting the skin of our body politic.

XJY

Does College need a new grace?

12 May 2009

Here is another everyday story of academic folk.

Our students at Newnham (or some of them, at least) are worried that the grace we use before dinner in Formal Hall is too Christian. Here we are, a college proud not to have a chapel (the only mainstream undergraduate college in Cambridge of which that is true) – and yet before formal dinners we are always thanking 'Jesum Christum dominum nostrum' (not to mention 'deum omnipotentem'), 'pro largitate tua …' etc. etc. A fair point, in a way.

So they brought to last week's college meeting an alternative grace for our consideration: 'Pro cibo inter esurientes, pro comitate inter desolatos, pro pace inter bellantes, gratias agimus' ('For food in a hungry world, for companionship in a world of loneliness, for peace in an age of violence, we give thanks').

Now a lot of work had gone into this, and there were no obvious grammatical howlers in the Latin. But, irreligious as I am, I just couldn't stomach it.

For a start, it was all terribly non-Classical, indeed medieval in tone. (True, agreed the Bursar – but then the Classical Romans didn't actually have grace, did they? And what we say already, would be more at home in a fifteenth-century cathedral than at Cicero's dinner table.) But worse, the undergraduates' rewrite was a classic case of disguising a load of well-meaning platitudes in some posh dead language, which was actually an insult to that dead language. The Beard

line was simple. Could we imagine getting up and saying this in English? No. Well, don't say it in Latin then. (At this point someone asked if one could say the *existing* grace in English with a straight face. Maybe not, I thought – but at least it has the virtue of hoary tradition.)

The debate got more complicated than this. Did the undergraduates want a *secular* grace or a *multi-faith* grace? If secular, then whom were they *thanking* in the new version? If it was simply a multi-faith version, then couldn't we just remove the 'Jesum Christum' bit. (Presumably Jews and Muslims and almost every faith could tolerate a 'deum omnipotentem'.)

After the meeting, we wondered if we shouldn't actually be thanking the cooks (or, to put it more crudely, those arguably exploited by us to bring us our nice food). But how would that go into Latin? 'Servi oppressi', suggested the Keeper of Antiquities at the Fitzwilliam (roughly translated as 'oppressed slaves'). Hardly a tactful way of thanking the staff, piped up the Bursar.

We then began to wonder if we needed formally to approve any form of grace at all. Maybe anyone who said grace should be able to say whatever form of grace they wanted. A *carte blanche* there, I thought, and suddenly warmed to a task I had previously shunned. And then there was the issue of the history of the existing grace. How long had it been said, and who had devised it? No one knew. (Some later research revealed that it had actually been framed by Jocelyn Toynbee, one of Newnham's most illustrious fellows ever – and a Catholic.)

Anyway, after this meeting, we went as usual to dinner. What grace would the Principal say?

She cleverly avoided the issue. 'Please be seated', she invited us.

Comments

'No one knew'. Do you mean to tell me that Newnham dons don't all keep a well-thumbed copy of *The College Graces of Oxford and Cambridge*, by Reginald Adams, by their bedsides? Shocking.

BEN WHITWORTH

'Everyday story of academic folk': no. 'Everyday story about
Cambridge': perhaps ...

RICHARD

Your students *understood* the grace?! Are you sure they're not
winding you up? All credit to your teaching, I'm sure, but at my college
it was a point of pride for the academic in question to reel it off as
quickly and pompously as possible. We are very fond of the college
ducks whom we enticed off Emmanuel, and as our grace starts
'quidquid nobis appositum est', it's called the 'quack quack grace'.

LUCY

It would make more sense to turn 'gratias agimus' into a
conditional: 'we would be grateful for food ...' This would then
involve entering into a new discourse with the Supreme Being.

ANTHONY ALCOCK

The Newnham 'Pro cibo' proposal strikes me as close in general
sentiment to the Selkirk Grace:
Some hae meat and canna eat,/ And some wad eat that want
it;/ But we hae meat, and we can eat,/ Sae let the Lord be
thankit.

RICHARD BARON

How about: 'To what we are about to consume we are perfectly
entitled'? An honest-to-goodness, graceless grace, that avoids all
the inter-faith bother. Would it add any relish to members' eating,
though?

NEIL JONES

Christianity banned

15 May 2009

It was perhaps (as has been pointed out to me) a little beyond propriety to blog about Newnham's internal discussions on its college grace. But I just couldn't resist. ('It is easier for a wise man to stifle a flame within his burning mouth than to keep *bona dicta* to himself', as the Roman poet Ennius said.) Besides, I thought college came rather well out of it, over all – students taking multiculturalism, multi-faith and the traditions of their institutions seriously, dons taking students' comments and suggestions seriously, the discussion going at the problem from every angle. Amusing from the outside it might have been, but it was feisty stuff – showcasing argumentative young women at a flourishing single-sex institution, not a load of Laura Ashley-clad wimps.

I feared the worst when the *Cambridge Evening News* rang up to get some more information, but was assured (!) that the story would be carefully and accurately handled, when it appeared in the Thursday edition. Well, the story itself was. But the headline (on the front page) ran 'GRACE BANNED' (which it certainly hadn't been).

It was only a matter of time before it was picked up by the *Mail*, *Express*, *Telegraph*, Jeremy Vine etc. etc.

How naive could I have been?

There was something in this story for every journalistic prejudice. The *Mail* managed to combine a hit at ungrateful students ('Students lucky enough to have won a place at Cambridge have plenty to be thankful for'), with a side-swipe at their anti-Christian sentiments (the Christian content of the traditional grace had 'proved too much for them'). This was followed by my objections to the Latin and some sensible words from the Senior Tutor. (Barely a mention of the non-denominational traditions of the college ... which was a big part of the students' point.) The comments on the article turned out to be a very mixed bag, from those cheering the abolition of the fetters of religion (yes, in the *Daily Mail*) to those lamenting the decline of Christian Britain (with a good bit of student-bashing mixed in).

The *Express* managed a cruder version of the above – 'Grace is ditched before dinner ...' (no it's not) – while the *Telegraph* and the *Times*'s Ruth Gledhill were predictably more measured, and researched. Ruth had even got Philip Howard to comment on the Latin ('I quite like its rhetorical triptych form. Not sure that Cicero would have liked those 'Inters') – and on the college ('Newnham is a college for high-minded ladies, and I dare say they want to think about peace and world poverty as well as pudding before sitting down' – sounds a bit Laura Ashley to me.)

All this has, of course, taken up a lot of time of the college officers, and as you can imagine, I am not exactly flavour of the month round here (though actually the publicity has been pretty good, by and large, and they had very nice pictures of the college).

Comments

I can't help feeling sorry for those members of Newnham reading who happen to like wearing Laura Ashley ... I understand the cliché you are working against, but you might choose not to go along with it, and rather acknowledge that young women who like floral dresses might also be serious intellectual beings with their own independent-minded take on the world.

RICHARD

Going to Oxford from Catholic Liverpool all those years ago, as I did, I was quite surprised to hear Latin being used by Protestants to thank the Omnipotent One for food on the table. We were told at school by the Jays not to read the Thirty-Nine Articles under any circumstances, so of course we did at the earliest opportunity. I was quite struck by the handsomeness of the English. I wonder why the 'clever men at Oxford' didn't produce a grace in English, which is an infinitely more beautiful language than Latin.

ANTHONY ALCOCK

Hold on, is it actually wrong to be thankful? I can see it being wrong to feel entitled – but thankful? 'True' thankfulness would produce generosity … I suppose the other option is just not to eat, etc. A possibility the morally ravaged have indeed explored, to their undying ethical credit.

Q

Being definitely not a Christian, I still took pleasure years ago from having to recite the college grace, that being the duty of scholars by rotation, a week at a time. Long Latin periods still resonate in my inner ear. And driving to work of a morning, I pass the west front of Westminster Abbey, where an English translation of much the same text is incised in stone letters about 6 inches high. These are experiences that you cannot buy, and one somehow feels that the young are misguided in pushing them away!

JEREMY STONE

Exam nightmares

12 June 2009

I have a new exam nightmare. For the last 35 years I've woken up every few weeks with the same one: I've just gone into the exam room and it's the wrong paper on the desk, or I've revised for the wrong paper, or the whole thing is written in some language I don't understand.

Anyway, I now have a new real-life nightmare. I don't get to the exam room to start the exam.

The Cambridge system is that one examiner from every 'board' turns up at every room in which one of their papers is to be sat – in case a student has a question, or has spotted a mistake, or whatever. Anyway I was down to turn up at the Corn Exchange on Monday morning, nine o'clock, to be there for the first thirty minutes of the Part IB Ancient History paper.

The truth is that I completely forgot.

It wasn't that I was doing something fun. I was in fact at home emailing my fellow examiner about how we were to divide up, and swap, the scripts between us. I just completely forgot I should be there in the Corn Exchange, all dressed up in my gown.

So at 9.20 a.m. (20 minutes after I should have been there) I had a call on my mobile from a member of the exam room staff, asking where I was. Actually I didn't quite get to the mobile in time, but soon enough, another call came via the Faculty. There wasn't a major problem, they explained. One student had had a question about the paper, but one which one of my heroic colleagues (who was there to supervise another paper) had been able to answer. But where was I, they wanted to know.

Answer: in my dressing gown at the kitchen table. After the call, I instantly got dressed and rushed off to the exam room (borrowing the husband's academic gown). When I got there, five minutes past the magic hour of 9.30, the chief invigilator was very nice to me (just like she is, I guess, to students who crack up or try to walk out).

I talked to the student who had had the question, then I chatted to the invigilator about the different behaviour of different students in different subjects. (Apparently students in some subjects will take a loo/fag break between every question they answer ...)

Then I got on my bike to go back to the office to wait for the scripts to be delivered (70 overall), and I've been marking ever since.

I live to fight another day, I think.

How do examiners mark exams?

15 June 2009

I wouldn't want to claim that exams are as bad for the markers as they are for the sitters. But the Cambridge Tripos is still a big investment of time and hard work for the dons. It's not just that you have to read each paper carefully (and I have spent more or less the whole of the last week on this, more than 12 hours a day). You have also to decide what principle of marking to adopt.

Put simply, if you are dealing with standard 'essay' papers, you can either go question by question (that is, mark all the answers to question 1, then all the answers to question 2 and so on) or you can go candidate by candidate (that is, mark all the answers from candidate A, then move on to candidate B and so on).

The advantage of the former is that you can compare the answers more directly and see more easily which candidates have got new or more interesting material.

About 20 years ago I was marking a set of Ancient History scripts in which the first candidate I marked referred to an anecdote about the fruit trees of the Athenian fifth-century politician Cimon. I was impressed. But when I discovered that at least 20 of the first 30 candidates had the same anecdote, I realised that it must have been banged on about in lectures.

The advantage of the candidate-by-candidate approach is that you can see the profile of an individual student's answer much more easily.

Over the years, I've developed a (time-consuming) compromise between the two. A rod for my own back, but fair to the students I think.

First of all I go through the papers, question by question. Then I go back to take a second look, candidate by candidate. I read each script quickly again, this time thinking of the overall performance of the individual student.

It *is* very time-consuming, but at least I can look the students in the eye. And that seems to me the basic principle of old-fashioned examining. There are all kinds of brutalities about it, but if you can face the candidate and feel OK about explaining why they got what they did – that's good enough for me.

Anyway what was I marking this year? Technically, I think I am not supposed to say. We are a communal *board* of examiners and take communal responsibility. But it wouldn't take long to guess that I have been marking Ancient History in Part IB (taken by most of our students at the end of their second year) – and indeed I have confessed so already.

These were the questions: two sections, three questions to be answered in three hours, one from each section. (I should say that these relate to the pre-defined syllabus of 'Paper 7' … this wasn't just a random set of questions.)

Section A
1. Was Demosthenes right to say that King Philip of Macedon was a threat to Greece?
2. 'The individual was the only thing that mattered.' Is this true of Greek politics and society in the fourth century BC?
3. Was the fourth-century Athenian Confederacy simply an imitation of the Athenian Empire in the fifth century?

4. Imagine you are a Roman senator in the reign of Hadrian. What would you see as the personal advantages and disadvantages of taking the governorship of the province of Asia?

5. 'Greek culture was more or less unaffected by Roman rule in the East.' Is this true?

6. How coercive was Roman rule in the Eastern provinces?

7. 'Religion at Rome was, in essence, a branch of politics – there was no such thing as private religious devotion as we know it.' Argue against this proposition.

8. Why did some Rome emperors punish Christians?

9. 'Goodness gracious me, I think I'm turning into a god' (Vespasian, on his death-bed). Can you explain why Romans took the deification of their emperors seriously?

Section B

10. Is all history writing about the present as much as about the past? (Answer with reference to at least two Greek or Roman historians.)

11. 'Exile makes good historians.' Is this true of Greek historians? Why?

12. Do Cicero's letters help us to understand his 'real' feelings and motivations?

13. 'Inscribed documents are particularly valuable because, unlike literary texts, they are free from bias.' Discuss.

14. 'It is very rare that a individual inscription has made much of a difference to our understanding of any aspect of Greek or Roman history.' Is this too gloomy an assessment of the value of epigraphy?

15. Can you ever reach a good understanding of an inscription without knowing its physical context and setting?

Remember: this exam is sat not by finalists, but by students at the end of their second year of a Classics degree (or, for those without Latin or Greek A level, at the end of their third year).

What do you think?

Comments

O please, Prof., don't tease …

What was the Cimon fruit tree anecdote? I didn't find it in the Wiki article (though I am now close to examining the lower half of the wine bottle – maybe I missed it?)

Indulge, do, just once, a lazy student …

PETER ADAMS

… aaah the Fruit Trees. As I remember it, the question was 'Unlike Rome, Classical Athens had no such thing as a system of patronage between rich and poor' … or something like that, but rather better expressed. The anecdote, again as I remember from Plutarch's *Life of Cimon* (I'm doing this without looking up!), said that Cimon used to keep his gardens open so that people could come and pick the fruit from his trees. Almost every damn candidate came out with this story and said (as I assume Dr Millett had in his lectures) that this was a passive form of patronage.

MARY BEARD

When I mark stuff, I usually divvy up the examinees into safe bets, teeterers and awkward buggers. I go through the safe bets to get an idea of the 'standard' and to allow for historical deviations, so to speak. Then I give the teeterers a real going-over and put the worst ones aside with a tentative plus or minus. Then I spend most of my time on the awkward buggers. The ones who bend the rules but might be right to do so. Or just plain twisted. Then back to the teeterers, who often seem a lot more rational and amenable after the awkward buggers. Then maybe back to the safe bets for a quick check if I've got time.

I've found that it usually takes about a paragraph or two to gauge the general standard of a candidate. And most are consistent. It's the inconsistent ones that bother me. And the consistently schizophrenic – the quintessential teeterers – the ones who write nice sentences (often a good sign), frinstance, but have little to say although they're often good at disguising this – having often learned the skill from their lecturers ;-). Or the less common wild and woolly writers who actually know what they're on about, but go barefoot to lectures and eat raw cabbage in the street (though these are usually the awkward buggers).

XJY

Wasn't it Arthur Lionel Smith – historian, Classicist, Master of Balliol – who got his wife to read scripts, interrupted by his calls for her to 'skip! skip!' once he thought he'd heard enough to judge each candidate?

These days examiners are required to complete a sheet for each script, outlining the reasons for the marks allocated. I've never heard of spouses helping.

DAVID MARTIN

This is my sort of advice for essay-writers: DO WRITE: 'Umberto Eco has argued that … ', 'This makes me think that … ', 'You will understand it better if you know the mythology' and 'Odysseus is crafty.' DON'T WRITE: 'It has been argued that … ', 'Therefore it can be said that … ', 'An understanding of the mythology is of benefit to the reader' and 'Thus it can be seen that the quality of craftiness could, to a certain extent, be applied at times to the character of Odysseus.'

MICHAEL BULLEY

I had a first-year student write to me once claiming to have been told at school that one ought, in essays, to preface statements with 'It might be argued that … ' or similar, and asking whether one ought to do the same at university. I suspect that this does sometimes happen, and explains why students sometimes write the equivalent of 'it could be argued that an elephant is larger than a mouse.'

RICHARD

There was actually a certain amount of culture shock involved in transferring from the English regime of weekly-essay-and-tutorial to the large lecture classes of a vast Middle Western campus a few years later. My first lecture class was on the Roman Republic and my TA a graduate student with a shiny new BA from a cut-glass women's college on the East Coast. I said to her that I had no idea how much the 80-odd students in the lecture class were taking in. 'That's easy', she said, 'set a pop quiz.' The morning I announced this was the nadir of my popularity as a lecturer. Fortunately one student saw the funny side. One of the questions was 'Who taught the Romans to foretell the future from the entrails of birds?' (expecting the answer 'The Etruscans'). The most memorable answer was 'Colonel Sanders.' My apologies if I have told this story before.

OLIVER NICHOLSON

An anecdote about Leofranc Holford-Strevens, now Classics editor at the OUP and a distinguished writer on ancient literature. Faced with an exam question whose rubric said, 'Translate the following … ', he elected to translate it into Serbo-Croat. There was no one in Oxford who could mark it, but they found someone at the University of London, who awarded an alpha. Since then, the rubric has read, 'Translate the following into English'. I suggest that someone now try a translation into Geordie English and see what happens.

The other concerns a student who spent the entire three hours on one question. He was given an alpha/gamma, and the alpha on the viva voce. Well, try it, chaps.

PAUL POTTS

I can answer A4.
a. Trousers haven't been invented.
b. Chesters Fort is freezing.

STEVE THE NEIGHBOUR

Graduation: no animals killed

29 June 2009

Our students graduated on Saturday. In Cambridge graduation lasts three days, from Thursday till Saturday. They go to pick up their degrees by college, in order of the date of foundation of the college (which means that Newnham, in 1871, comes at the beginning of the last day).

I never go to the ceremony itself. In fact I have never been to a graduation ceremony at all, not even my own – for any of my degrees (I just got the certificate through the post, *in absentia* as the phrase is). When I was first graduating with my BA, I just couldn't face all the rituals – the dressing up in the fur-lined hood, the clasping the fingers of the 'praelector', the Latin and the hand-clasping with the vice-chancellor (or the VC's deputy – the top dog understandably doesn't sit in the Senate House for three days presiding over this).

I also couldn't face organising the whole show for a pair of divorced parents (they weren't technically divorced, as it turned out – my Dad had lost interest in the whole proceedings after the decree nisi and had never bothered to apply for the decree absolute, despite reminders from his solicitors … but they were divorced in spirit). I told both of them a real whopper: graduation wasn't any longer what most people did, it was just for the blazer brigade.

It is now one of my biggest regrets. At the cost of a little embarrassment to MB and some deft negotiation of parental squabbling, I could have given them a really proud and memorable day. So now when any student says to me that they

don't fancy it, I try my hardest to persuade them to go through
with it.

And I always try to go to the party that Newnham lays on
for every one after the ceremony itself.

It is, I guess, much as it always has been – loads of young
women in fur-lined hoods, loads of beaming mums and dads
(who have a capacity to be delighted even when the offspring
didn't do quite as well as they might secretly have hoped) and
lashings of bubbly. (Don't tell the *Telegraph*: I'm pretty sure the
students pay anyway!) My pleasant job – and it really is fun – is
to track down my students and to meet their parents, usually
for the first time.

Only once in 25 years has any parent complained about
anything. They are mostly very grateful and impressed for
what we offer (especially for the personal attention that senior
academics give to their daughters) – and they are only too
happy to share unbloggable insights into their offspring, which
one is glad one hadn't known before!

It could all have been a ceremony taking place 50 years ago.
Except for a few things. We now have a stall selling the college
merchandise to the graduands and their relations. (Anyone for
a teddy with a Newnham scarf or jumper?) And the fur hoods
are now not real but safely synthetic. Indeed the programme
of the ceremony in the senate house explicitly reassures the
worried audience that no animals have been killed in the
making of this graduation ceremony.

Well, not quite. One of my students had got hold of an
old hood, which indeed had been made out of real bunny (or
whatever). And I have to say that it looked much more elegant.
It was a soft dusky cream, not the bright polyester-feel white of
the synthetic versions, which moult all over the place and get
full of static.

OK, to kit them all out with the real version could not possibly be worth a mass cull of the rabbit population (even supposing the animal-friendly students would tolerate it) – but it would certainly be an aesthetic improvement.

Comments

The order in which colleges present their candidates for degrees is: King's (founded 1441), Trinity (founded 1546), St John's (founded 1511), followed by the other colleges in order of their foundation, from Peterhouse (founded 1284) onwards (Ordinances of the University of Cambridge, Chapter 2, Section 10.12).

Yours pedantically, Nick Denyer, Praelector and Father of Trinity College

NICHOLAS DENYER

As a prole who did two degrees at Oxford, and reluctantly attended one degree ceremony belatedly to please my parents (as I am the first of my family to go on in education beyond the age of 14, they had been disappointed when I didn't take the first one), I could not bear the kowtowing and obsequiousness before the reactionary etc. I surfed through my ceremony on a wave of class hatred for a system which was invented so that people like me couldn't get in, by and large.

I hoped it meant something that the daughter of a binman and a cleaner was being hectored in Latin in the Sheldonian, but, realistically, probably not a lot.

E LONGLEY

You lot have had it easy! Try taking a degree while working full-time, running a home, and in many cases, bringing up children. Your moment in the sun is priceless. A degree ceremony, dressed in that hard-won robe, and without the 'silly hat' (a much debated issue!) is the culmination of many years study, often in isolation, and not to be missed. You are surrounded by people who have been through the same experiences, and who are, to a man/woman, raising the roof with their clapping and cheering. My BA ceremony was presided over by our Chancellor, 'our Betty', the wonderful Betty Boothroyd. I wouldn't have missed it for the world.

JACKIE

Was Alexander the Great a Slav?

3 July 2009

This is a row I really don't get. Over the last few years FYROM (the Former Yugoslav Republic of Macedonia) has been investing heavily in Alexander the Great. FYROM's main airport is now called 'Alexander the Great Airport' (better than 'John Lennon' or 'Bob Hope' airports, you might think). A vast statue of Alexander (eight storeys high, apparently) is planned for the centre of Skopje. And the word on the street is that Alexander was a Slav.

This seems to me to be, at best, rather touching. It's nice to think that there is still enough symbolic life in this drunken juvenile thug that someone *wants* him for their nation. At worst, it is faintly silly. The antecedents of Alexander are a bit murky, but in truth there isn't a cat in hell's chance that he was a Slav. I can see also that it could be a bit annoying to some Greeks who might want to try to claim Alexander for themselves (this is a better claim than the Slavic one, but not exactly cast-iron).

But what on earth has persuaded over 300 Classical scholars (several of whom are good friends of mine) to sign a letter to President Obama (copy to Mrs Clinton et al.) asking him to intervene personally to clear up this FYROM historical travesty.

I hope Obama has got some more important wrongs to right. But supposing that he has had a minute to look at this missive, I trust that he won't be won over by the outraged arguments.

The territory of FYROM, they point out, is more strictly that of ancient Paionia, not Macedonia. (Fair enough, but so what – we don't stop Northern Ireland calling itself part of Great Britain, even though it wasn't part of ancient Britannia.) The other arguments in the letter are decidedly dodgier, and not the kind of thing that the learned signatories would (I hope) give high marks to in an undergraduate essay.

There is the usual stuff about how Alexander's ancestors must have been Greek as they competed in the Olympic Games. (In fact there was originally some dispute at the time about whether they were, or were not, Greek enough to qualify.) But the worst argument is the claim that 'the Macedonians traced their ancestry to Argos', and so were bona fide, not FYROM-style, Greeks. Well, of course the Macedonians said that. It was a convenient and self-serving *myth*, no truer than the Athenians' claim that they were born from the soil of Athens.

By putting their names to this rubbish, I can't help feeling that my friends are stooping to exactly the kind of nationalism that they are trying to oppose. If you really wanted to undermine the Macedonian claims, wouldn't it be better (and academically more credible) simply to laugh at them and just refuse to take them seriously?

Comments

This post attracted more comments than any other, most berating me for being pro-Greek or anti-Greek, pro-FYROM or anti-FYROM: 'I am amazed that a professor at Cambridge can try to promote her views without any proof'; 'Mary Beard has been drinking too much ouzo as her pro-Greek stance is quite pathetic.' And so on. A few struck a different note:

Unless I remember wrongly, it was clearly established that the Ptolemies and the Macedonian royal family were in fact American: hence their invasion of the whole Middle East, and the large number of Philadelphias, Pellas etc. in the USA.

The point that Philip must have been Greek because of his activities at Delphi is particularly laughable: since he had established himself as the strongest military power in Greece at the time, there was little enough the other Greeks could do about it, and his keenness to gain a prominent role at the sanctuary reflects his only-dubiously-Greek status.

It's quite alarming how many distinguished scholars are willing to sign up to this crap. However, since President Obama's personal background combines elements from Kenya, Hawaii, Indonesia and he is nevertheless quite clearly an American, I don't imagine he will take this 'because of what happened in the fourth century BC' model of ethnicity very seriously.

RICHARD

Alexander's father was a snake (Plut. *Alex*. ii,4; Justin xi.11.3; Q.Curt. I)

PL

The contrast between the impressive list of names and the buffoonishness of the sentiments expressed therein is indeed striking. This is a question of contemporary politonymy, and none of the signatories seems to have addressed the question from this point of view, assuming wrongly as they do that their Alexanderological expertise gives them authority to pontificate on modern geopolitics. But the problem is not 'was Alexander a

Slav?' or 'were ancient Macedonians Greeks?', but 'how are modern state names authorized?' Are there other cases of states assuming a name previously given to a province of another country? And the answer is yes. Luxembourg is the name both of a province of Belgium and an independent state, Moldova a region of Romania and a contiguous independent republic. Nobody has any problem figuring that an older region turned into two units.

SW FOSKA

Ten Latin quotes for the underground

5 July 2009

Last week it was reported that the drivers on the Piccadilly line would be adding some well-chosen quotes to their announcements on the underground: 'Hell is other people', 'Beauty will save the world' and other appropriate thoughts for a commuting journey.

Surely, with Boris Johnson as mayor, there ought to be some real Latin among the anglophone platitudes. Indeed, a surprising number of the best-known Latin quotes turn out to be surprisingly appropriate for the journey to work. In no particular order:

1. '**perfer et obdura! dolor hic tibi proderit olim**' – or 'Be patient and put up with it; one day this pain will pay dividends.' That's Ovid (*Amores* III, XIa) reflecting on the insults of his mistress – but fits well enough for the rush-hour commute.

2. '**quousque tandem abutere, Catilina, patientia nostra**' – or 'How long, Catiline, will you abuse our patience?'. The famous first line of Cicero's first speech against Catiline, attacking the would-be revolutionary (or innocent stooge) Catiline. But you can substitute any adversary for Catiline. 'quousque tandem abutere, Boris, patientia nostra?'

3. '**arma virumque cano**' – or 'Arms and the man I sing'. The most famous line in the whole of Latin poetry, the first line of the first book of Virgil's *Aeneid*. Though Virgil didn't exactly mean the arms of the man digging into your side,

as you're stuck in the tunnel between Covent Garden and Leicester Square.

4. **'amantium irae amoris integratio est'** – or 'Lovers' quarrels are the renewal of love' (that's from Terence's comedy *The Woman of Andros*, 555). Something to cheer you up after a bad night.

5. **'medio tutissimus ibis'** – or 'You'll go safest in the middle', from Ovid, *Metamorphoses* II, 137. Advice to Phaethon, who was about – disastrously – to drive the chariot of the sun. Probably not much better advice on the underground.

6. **'audacibus annue coeptis'** – or 'Look with favour on a bold start' (as in Virgil, *Georgics* 1, 40). You could translate as – make for the tube door first, and don't worry about the elderly, disabled or women with buggies.

7. **'nemo enim fere saltat sobrius, nisi forte insanus'** – or 'No one dances sober, unless maybe he's mad' (Cicero, *Pro Murena* 6, 13). More memories of last night.

8. **'nil desperandum'** – or 'don't despair about anything' (Horace, *Odes* I, 7, 27). Self-explanatory for the rush-hour journey, but hard advice to follow.

9. Better perhaps would be **'nunc est bibendum'** – or 'Now is the time to drink' (Horace, *Odes* I, 37, 1 – in the original celebrating the death of Cleopatra).

10. **'capax imperii nisi imperavisset'** – or 'capable of ruling if he hadn't ruled' (or roughly, 'he had a great future behind him'). This is what Tacitus had to say of the emperor Galba after his speedy assassination.

Too soon to tell if Boris has a great future behind him!

Comments

More Virgil: The encouraging *'Forsan et haec olim meminisse juvabit'* – 'Perhaps even all this will one day be a happy memory' (Aeneas cheering up his companions after their shipwreck on a forbidding coast). Or *'Hic labor, hic opus est'* – 'This the labour, here the work to be achieved' (the Cumaean Sibyl telling Aeneas that it's the coming back alive from the world of the dead, not the going down there, that is the hard part).

PL

For those who have to use the Northern line:
'Nox est perpetua una dormienda' … (Catullus)
['An eternal night – all you can do is sleep through it']

ANNA

It would be enough if the announcements were intelligible. I was once on the tube with a French person whose English was quite good and I persuaded him, the French being gullible, that the announcement that had just been made was in Hungarian and was an example of London Transport's commitment to multiculturalism.

MICHAEL BULLEY

How about *'cave hiatum'* – mind the gap!

ANDYC

'Odi profanum vulgus et arceo'. Horace. I'm surprised no one else has come up with this. 'I hate the common mob and keep them at arm's length'.

MICHAEL BENNETT

Why is that the subject of Latin brings out the Radio 4 in people?
ANTHONY ALCOCK

There's the old anecdote of a graffiti written when Boston Latin
High School was closed because a severe snowstorm had closed
the subway. 'Sick Transit. Glorious Monday!'
NICK NUSSBAUM

What were job references like in the old days?

20 July 2009

Anyone who has been involved in academic job interviews and selection – especially for early career posts – knows how important the references are. The candidates in question probably have very few publications that you can read; you need a supportive but honest assessment of strengths and weaknesses from someone who knows them.

Anyone who has *recently* been involved will also know how difficult it is to get a supportive but honest assessment. The current rhetoric is of unadulterated praise, sometimes (I fear) laughably dishonest. It's worse among American referees, but the Brits are fast catching up. In writing the instructions to referees for our college research fellowship competition a few years ago, I added some phrase to the effect of 'an unadulterated eulogy will not help your candidate'. I can't say that it had much effect among the persistent offenders.

I always vow to write to these with a few simple queries. 'Could you please compare Dr Y, whom you rate this year as 'the most brilliant student you have ever taught', with Dr Z, of whom you said the same last year. It would help the committee to know which in your view was absolutely *the* most brilliant.' But I never quite get round to it.

Anyway, clearing out my study, I found some references for a Cambridge job, advertised and appointed well over 20 years ago.

They were both better and worse than their modern equivalent.

As they are so old, and as some of the candidates – let alone the referees – are long dead, I think it is OK to give you some anonymised quotes from these. (I have changed anything that could possibly, even at this distance, lead to identification – including gender.)

For a start, what was worse than now?

That's simple: the sexism. For almost every married woman in the pack, the referee felt bound to say that she was 'happily married' (how did they know – and would we have looked worse on an imminent divorcee, anyway?), and that the husband was very happy for his wife to have a job. A few launched into the childcare arrangements, while suggesting that we would obviously want to talk more about this at the interview. Thank God that's now illegal.

But these references were mostly a lot more helpful than today's; they were prepared to talk about the weaknesses of the candidates and occasionally ventured a joke or two.

Try this for an alert to a weakness: 'First a criticism. Repetitiveness – no, rather verbosity. On a random sample of pages I thought that I could cut about 10% merely by verbal pruning. But X is well aware of this and is at the moment practising a little discipline.'

Or this for a comment on the candidate's match to the job description: 'He is not the first person that I would have thought of for this particular post ... although he would be competent to discharge it.'

Or this: 'I do not think he has done much, if any, teaching, and I suspect he is not particularly gifted as a teacher. I have found him rather diffident and unforthcoming in conversation. I would advise an interviewing committee, and

I believe he deserves to be interviewed, to concentrate its attention on this area.'

Or this for a warning note: 'As an undergraduate she showed a tendency to indulge a taste for slightly eccentric philological speculation. I have no doubt ... that this tendency is now well under control.'

Then again, try this for a compliment: 'I've never had any reason to suspect him of bluff or one-upmanship even in the sort of conversation where relatively sober scholars are liable to overbid their hands.'

Or this: 'If he were a bit flashier at interview, he would have got some kind of job by now, I feel.'

And how about this for support, but not yet: 'She sometimes has so many ideas at once, that she is not quite sure which to talk about first ... I am convinced that she will be successful soon when she applies for a research fellowship. I am not at all sure that she should at this stage of her career take a teaching post.'

True, you might say that all this was old school prejudice, or unsupported assertion, or self-promoting cleverness on the part of the referee. But compared to the sewers of praise you find now, it was jolly helpful.

Comments

The Chichele Professor of Modern History in the University of Oxford in the 1980s sent a handwritten reference for a friend applying for posts in the USA. It read in full: 'He is a sound man.' It did not result in any interviews. The Chichele Professor rightly admired my friend's work.

I am sorry that Mary believes that anonymity is a virtue in these stories.

OH FLACK

'He is a sound man'. Perhaps the Americans thought that 'he' worked in a recording studio.

ANTHONY ALCOCK

It occurs to me, Mary, that, in fact, you are breaching the Data Protection Act by retaining information relating to candidates long after a reasonable length of time has elapsed from the date of the recruitment exercise.

Pedant heaven, here.

JANE

Jane. Is that so – given that these documents had no electronic form and so are not and never have been 'data' within the terms of the act?? If it WERE the case, I would count it another reason to feel suspicious of the act (or the way it is applied).

MARY BEARD

The data doesn't have to be in electronic form. It can be part of 'a relevant filing system' defined as data held 'in such a way that specific information relating to a particular individual is readily accessible'. Pedant heaven, as Jane says! But as far as I understand it, it's not illegal to retain the data, so long as the 'data subject' has access to it.

SW FOSKA

On data protection, I'm OK then. To be lingering in the bottom of an old box in a carrier bag, in which they must have been carried to and from the shortlisting meeting … doesn't really count as 'a relevant filing system'!

And they are in the process of destruction. But where does this leave proper scholarly archiving of what will be historic documents?

MARY BEARD

Steven Pinker suggests that the perfect negative reference would read: 'X is very punctual and has a charming wife.'

CSRSTER

WHO says British universities are complacent?

3 August 2009

Almost every newspaper in the UK today had a story about the failings of universities. A parliamentary inquiry, they said, had branded British universities as complacent, unwilling to justify their standards to outside scrutiny, unable to justify the fact that (e.g.) the proportion of firsts had risen significantly in the last decade or so.

As usual, if you actually look at the original report from which all this comes (not just the press release), the story is rather different. In this case, it is both better and worse than the newspaper reports make out.

Better? Well, the 'Students and Universities' report of the House of Commons' Innovation, Universities, Science and Skills Committee has some pretty harsh words for the government. It criticises the idea that more university places can be made available without extra funding. It queries the effect of so much emphasis on research output (writ in stone by the Research Assessment Exercise). And it recommends that the government takes a hard look at school education before simply bashing the universities (the standard response to any question of aspiration, social mobility etc. etc.). So far, so good.

But there is worse in the small print.

As I read this document, I asked myself where the Committee had been for the last 20 years. There are a series of recommendations which urge greater cooperation between universities and schools 'to facilitate widening participation in higher education'.

Absolutely. But do they not know that, where I come from, this is happening already? Indeed I am, at this minute, proudly carrying round in my bag a copy of a letter from a retiring teacher at both independent and maintained schools – thanking my own Faculty for all the hard work and input we have given to his/her schools over the last 30 years.

Likewise, we have for years been taking 'context' into account in the process of admitting students – another thing they seem to think of as radical and rare.

Then there is all the silly stuff about how badly we compare with the student experience at universities in Europe and the USA. According to this report, our students study (including library time) less than students in other European countries. And their 30 hours per week is just half the 60 hours that students in the USA claim to study. At this point, anyone who has experience of university teaching in the USA and Europe must say that they cannot have been comparing like for like.

So who are 'they', and how did they do the comparisons? And where was Cambridge in all this?

'They' were the 'Innovation, Universities, Science and Skills' parliamentary committee, 13 of them (11 men and 2 women). And to produce this report they had met just nine times to hear 'evidence', seven times in London and once in Liverpool and Oxford. They also went once to Washington to discover about US universities.

This begins to explain why they hadn't caught up with the kind of university experience that is my bread and butter. They had not come to Cambridge once, nor did they hear oral evidence from any Cambridge student or academic in post.

(Maybe we could have written in, but didn't – perhaps because we were too busy.) Their special advisers were all those who worked in research into higher education (not an ordinary practitioner among them).

And the only access they had to any comparative material from overseas was written statistics or their single trip to Washington. Only one member of the committee (Gordon Marsden) had any experience of working or studying in an American university. None had experience of a European campus. I have both. And to me it seems absolutely preposterous to suggest that (whatever the current difficulties of the UK system) the undergraduate experience elsewhere is better.

If you are worried about assured standards in the UK, try looking at the USA – where the grades for each course are normally given by the lecturer who taught the class, and by no one else. When these guys criticised our system, with its double marking *and* external examiners, did they realise that? And didn't they realise how much of the teaching in elite universities in the States was done by postgraduate students, when they criticised that aspect of UK universities?

Meanwhile, as Cambridge kept quiet, others in the academy made their views very well known to the committee. Michael Arthur, the Vice-Chancellor of Leeds, keeps cropping up in the report – and being patted on the back for 'innovations' that have been common in Cambridge (or at least in my subject in college) for years … a specific programme of support for those students from non-traditional backgrounds etc. etc. Presumably he wrote in vociferously, and no one really knew whether his innovations were innovations or not?

And they didn't always check out whether he was right. He claimed that 9 members of the committee were graduates of

'Russell Group' universities. I could only make that 7 members. But I did notice that only 2 out of 13 had done Arts subjects (unless Rob Wilson did – whose degree I can't discover). Is that significant in their pushing of Science?

I don't mind a group of MPs doing a quick raid into higher education. Indeed I am rather pleased that they do. I do mind the rest of the country imagining that this is well researched and well founded. In fact this is precisely the kind of stuff I would warn my students against.

Comments

Mary B's quite wrong on this.

While Cambridge and one or two others may be exceptions to the general UK – and others in Europe – rule, experience on both sides of the Atlantic does indeed indicate to me that US students do about twice as much work as British students. Even in the case of Cambridge and similar, where the work load is higher, comparing like for like, US students at places like Harvard do a whole lot more work – reading, writing, discussion groups etc. – than those at Cambridge.

MB also notes that in the US system (in many cases) 'the grades for each course are normally given by the lecturer who taught the class, and by no one else'. The fact is that the burden of administering second gradings and external examining is vastly out of proportion to the gains accruing to students from them. In many UK-style universities weeks are spent on these processes, where it would be much better to, yes, let the lecturer who taught the course just grade the papers and have done with it.

OTTO

Otto – I find it slightly incredible that US students work on average twice as hard as UK students. First, I probably spend 7 hours a day working during term time. Now, I'm a history student and thus tend to have a much lighter work load than some of my scientist friends who are in labs 9–5 and then work in the evening to finish tutorial sheets. Let's say they do 10 hours a day of work in the week and 7 at weekends. So my question is: what physiological difference do US students have which some how allows them to survive on 4 hours a day for sleep and sustenance?

JOSH

I think the question of workload is irrelevant. You wouldn't say it was because he worked many hours that Mozart ended up a good composer. He was because he was. Whatever the demands made on the student, the university must be judged by the effect they have, and not in terms of the demands themselves, such as the number of contact hours and so on.

MICHAEL BULLEY

Ten things you shouldn't believe about A levels

20 August 2009

It's the A level season again, and everyone feels they have a right to pontificate on the state of the nation's youth, the failings/successes of education etc. etc. That includes me.

Here is my self-opinionated Top Ten of what *not* to believe:

1. A levels are getting easier.

No, they are not. They are different from what we used to do, and they don't test some of the skills that I personally value highly ('open-ended' essay writing, for example). But the hard work required is just as it ever was.

2. More students get A grades because they are now better taught.

No, I'm not saying teaching isn't better now. (I honestly don't know.) But I strongly suspect that more students are getting As because today's A levels have much clearer criteria, towards which it is easier to work (contrary to open-ended essays).

3. More students get A grades because they are cleverer than they used to be.

No, see 2 – but I do suspect that they work harder, partly because it can be easier to work harder towards clear criteria. (Personally I think that this is lousy training for later, but that's another story.)

4. Some A levels are easier than others.
Well, this is a bit of a no and yes. I would tend to rate someone
more highly for future academic success if they had As in
Latin, Maths and Further Maths … than if they had As in
(say) Media Studies, Health and Social Care, and Sport Studies
(though I could be wrong). But there isn't a single spectrum
here. The kid who gets a top A in Further Maths might be
completely hopeless at Media Studies.

**5. The brightest kids are those ones who manage to clock up
As in six or seven subjects at A level.**
No way. This is the A level equivalent of stamp collecting. No
one ever needs more than four A levels – and if that leaves
them any free time, it would be the best thing intellectually to
read novels, go to the movies … and grow up.

**6. It is the job of the best universities to take into
account that many disadvantaged state schools tend to
underestimate their pupils' A level grades when they make
predictions.**
That, at least, is what John Dunford, head of the Association
of School and College Leaders, has been reported as saying.
No it isn't – or only in part. It would be more to the point if he
got his Association to do something to rectify the problem at
school level.

**7. Things will be put right if we reintroduce the old-style
essay-writing exam.**
Not entirely. Exams are only as good as the examiners. The
new-style 'clear-criteria' exam can be marked by the relatively
inexperienced (that's in part why they were invented). In
the old days you could have a more open-ended essay style
of question, because you had relatively few candidates and

a cadre of experienced examiners. Where will you find enough experienced examiners to take this on … ?

8. The International Baccalaureate is much better than A levels.

No. The grass on the other side always looks greener, but if we were to go over to this *en bloc*, you'd find just as many complaints. The breadth will be good for some but not for others. There is no quick fix.

9. It is better for the country if more kids take Science and Maths at A levels (according to Schools Minister Iain Wright).

No – not necessarily. Or only if they want to, and that is where their talents lie. In the long term (and even in the short term, I suspect) kids well educated in any subject are good for the country's success and economy. Forcing them to do science only produces unwilling and bad scientists.

10. Geniuses pass their A levels at a preternaturally young age. (There were a pair of eight-year-old twins this year, I believe, who got a B and a C in Advanced Maths.)

No, no, no. Maybe they are clever, but the reason they have had this exam inflicted on them is that they have preternaturally pushy parents.

Comments

The whole business of marking, per se, seems desperately flawed. And yet how to get along without it? Like the opposite sex, there's no living with it and no living without it – only it's also impossible to fall in love with.

PL

I disagree with all this. The clear criteria thing is obviously what is needed – no woolly fluff. Fax fax fax and stubby forefingers.

'Teachers' are the labourers of the system, brute sluggers hacking off the coal – it's the sorters and refiners and pit-owners who give the process value – and make the coal useful for the productive sector so it can produce the things we need.

All this open-ended sludge and 'whole man' crap is just the exception that proves the rule that where there's muck there's money.

XJY

And one thing to *believe* about A levels: 50% of A levels taken in private schools are awarded a grade A compared to 20% in state comprehensives. And Mary believes that Cambridge does not need to do anything about this.

STATE

State – it is not Cambridge's job to set to rights the shortcomings of the state school system. If they take that on as a matter of course, and keep making allowances, there is no incentive for improvement. I, as someone with grandchildren in the state system, just wish that the powers that be could differentiate between 'equality' and 'equality of opportunity', and not try to reduce everybody to the lowest common denominator. The result is that somebody else has to pick up the pieces, and teach the basic skills at 18 that should have been honed by the time A levels come around.

JACKIE

Sex with students? Is Terence Kealey as misunderstood as Juvenal?

24 September 2009

A few weeks ago I had an email from a friend who works on *Times Higher Education* (*THE*) asking if I would contribute 500 words to their forthcoming feature on 'The Seven Deadly Sins of the Academy'.

I was tempted, but as my favourite sins (notably sartorial inelegance and procrastination) had already been taken, I gave it a miss. And when the article actually appeared last week, I hardly had time to look at it (except to notice a cheap pot shot at the complacency of nineteenth-century Classics by the multi-talented Simon Blackburn – who should, in this case, have known better).

I hadn't realised that there was a storm about Terence Kealey's piece on 'Lust', till I got an email from a man on the *Evening Standard*, asking me if I would like to comment on it – largely because I had past 'form' on the issue of sex between students and university teachers. So I took a look at it.

'Clark Kerr' it began, 'the president of the University of California from 1958–1967, used to describe his job as providing sex for the students, car parking for the faculty and football for the alumni. But what happens when the natural order is disrupted by faculty members who, on parking their cars, head for the students' bedroom ... Why do universities pullulate with transgressive intercourse? ... The fault lies with the females.'

'The myth is', he went on, 'that an affair between a student and her academic lover represents an abuse of power. What power? Thanks to the accountability imposed by the Quality Assurance Agency the days are gone when a scholar could trade sex for upgrades.' Anyway he conceded, 'Normal girls ... will abjure their lecturers for the company of their peers, but nonetheless most male lecturers know that most years there will be a girl in class who flashes her admiration ... what to do? Enjoy her! She's a perk. She doesn't yet know that you are only Casaubon to her Dorothea ... and she will flaunt you her curves. Which you should admire daily to spice up your sex, nightly, with the wife.'

It was instantly clear to me that this was SATIRE. So I replied in these terms:

'I have looked at the Kealey piece ... and thought it wicked satire, but certainly satire, which is of course always meant to be offensive, thought-provoking, and often intended to rebound on the very views it satirises ... that's the point ... try Juvenal, if you want an ancient precedent.'

I then looked round the web to find all kinds of huffing and puffing about Kealey, the Vice-Chancellor of the University of Buckingham, who regards sex with students as a 'perk' of the academic profession. The *Mail* even managed to drag in an old article of mine which referred to 'the erotics of pedagogy'.

Taking several more careful looks at the Kealey piece, I was left in no doubt that he was aiming his darts at the ways crude sexual exploitation of female students gets justified, by satirically mimicking the locker-room style in which it is discussed. Come on everyone, NO VICE-CHANCELLOR (not even of Buckingham) calls women students a 'perk' unless satirically (and aiming a dart at precisely those assumptions). Honest.

It was however a dreadful experience looking not only at the press reports of all this but also the comments of the *THE* website (some of which were presumably written by academics, who showed no ability to read or understand satire *at all* … maybe they were all computer scientists, but I rather doubt it). To be fair, a few did make the plea for humour and satire. But not many.

'It is appalling that *THE* permitted the deeply offensive comments about female undergraduates … to appear in its pages', said 'gobsmacked'.

'Anyone who thinks that thinks that female students are there in the classroom expressly as objects of the instructors' viewing pleasure needs to retire (please)', opined 'sg'.

'What is most shocking is the disrespect to his wife', added 'Colemar'.

'Smelling of old person like a pee-soaked slipper', quipped (?) 'Dave'.

God help the students these people (and the all the others like them) teach. I would much rather have instruction from Kealey myself.

The issue here is, of course (though hardly anyone observed this), the perennial problem of fixing the 'ideology' of satire. When Roman Juvenal huffs and puffs about the immorality of his own late first-/early second-century Rome, is he the conservative misogynist that he superficially seems to be, or is he holding up those views for ridicule? In Juvenal's case almost certainly the latter.

Likewise with the 1960s' comic anti-hero Alf Garnett. Was he pillorying racism, or making it easier to condone?

The trouble with satire, as poor Kealey has found, is that the literal-minded are always liable not to get it. And the satirist is inadvertently taken to support the very views s/he is attacking.

(The very cynical therefore may always suspect double bluff – but I don't, here.)

Comments

The reference to Alf Garnett is well made. I was horrified a couple of years ago to hear a group of people involved in TV light entertainment, in a TV discussion, agreeing emphatically that it would be unthinkable nowadays to have a comedy programme with a character expressing views like Alf Garnett's. Maybe they were afraid modern audiences wouldn't grasp it was satire. If so, that's a sad thought about modern sensibilities. But, in fact, I got the impression they themselves hadn't grasped it was satire. You need iron in your body, but you also need irony.

MICHAEL BULLEY

So as a computer scientist who is interested in history and the Classics, and reads and writes Latin, and even has read some of your books, can I ask why the gratuitous swipe at computer scientists?

In my experience, the popular image of geeky computer scientist and well-rounded Classicist is a myth. Most computer scientists are avid fans of history and the humanities, which they pursue as a side interest while working with IT in their jobs. Most Classicists OTOH know their field and little else, and their IT expertise goes as far as buying books at Amazon and writing papers in Word.

TAYLOR

One of the downsides, surely, of being a university vice-chancellor is that you don't get to make satirical comments about issues like your lecturers perving on your students. Who cares if it's satire?

LUCY

Rule Number One in Public Rhetoric: NO IRONY!!!

Tom Lehrer was right, as always: 'political satire became obsolete when Henry Kissinger was awarded the Nobel Prize.'

XJY

Satire is never devoid of ethical undercurrents and often has an instructive purpose. An analogous case: Matthew Parris writes in the *Times* about 18 months back: 'Let's decapitate cyclists, they are so naff in their lycra ha ha ha.' Cyclists who complained were sneered at that they lacked a sense of humour etc. But in a world where real people string wire across cycle paths and think this funny, Parris's article seemed to me to be as authentic a case of incitement to violence as an author of a legal textbook could wish for. Its satirical intent is no alibi for its consequences. Is not the same logic at work here?

SW FOSKA

It certainly is difficult to 'fix the ideology' of satire and of ironic expression: that's one of the reasons why people like the VC of the University of Bucks adopt 'defensive irony' as a way of trying to have their cake and eat it: they hope to find a way to enjoy their 'transgressive' expressions while disowning responsibility for them. If it's done well, people tend to find it amusing and witty. But, as Dave already observed, if it's done badly, as in this case it was, it makes the writer (or speaker) look like a dickhead.

I mean the last word ironically, of course …

RICHARD

Hmmm, nothing on male students and female academics, or
indeed on same-sex relationships. There is a PhD in this for
someone. But perhaps the best practical solution is for the QAA
and their ilk to devise a proper protocol for lecturer–student
relationships, with a formal plan for starting and managing
each one, clear objectives and external monitoring to ensure
consistency in the relationships within and across institutions. (If it
happens, you read it here first.)

RICHARD BARON

Did *Portnoy's Complaint* deserve the 'Booker Prize'?

18 October 2009

When I was a teenager, I took Philip Roth's *Portnoy's Complaint* to school in my satchel, in the hope – I think – of having it discovered by some prudish teacher and provoking an argument about freedom of speech and sexual expression (and also to show how hip I was). My mother, I remember, requested it from the local library, for similar – if slightly more grown-up – reasons.

Until a few weeks ago I couldn't remember much about it, apart from the description of masturbation with the piece of liver. Presumably that's what everyone remembers.

I have, however, recently re-read it. It wasn't a happy experience. What was the virtue or merit of a 200-and-something page monologue of repetitive, blokeish sexual fantasy, preoccupied with the pleasures and guilt of masturbation (or alternatively with exploitative sex with exploited women ... or if not sex, then constipation and other aspects of the 'lower bodily stratum', as Bakhtin would have put it)? I wasn't shocked. In fact, the liver bit was quite coyly done, and the use of a cored apple for the same purpose was a rather underwhelming image. It was the sheer self-indulgence of the book that was so irritating.

For a moment the horrible thought came to me that this really was what men thought about all the time – that this was

a true exposé of 'what men were like'. If so, I thought it was
probably better not to know.

The reason for putting myself through this literary
torture was that I had agreed to be a panellist/judge on the
Cheltenham Literary Festival's Booker event – going back to
the novels published in 1969, to give a retrospective Booker
prize. In reality, the novels published in 1969 were up for the
(second) Booker in 1970. The winner was Bernice Rubens's
The Elected Member. But we were choosing between *Portnoy*
(supported by John Walsh), Graham Greene's *Travels with
my Aunt* (supported by Kate Adie), Margaret Atwood's *The
Edible Woman* (supported by Erica Wagner) and John Fowles's
French Lieutenant's Woman (mine). None of these had been
in the running for the original prize. *Portnoy* was ineligible as
Roth is American. Greene had refused to be considered. The
Atwood had in 1969 only been published in Canada, so hadn't
really made it on to the radar here. And the Fowles didn't
get anywhere. (The word on the street is that it was totally
scuppered by Rebecca West, who was one of the judges.)

So who won our 40 years on prize?

First to be eliminated was *The Edible Woman*. Erica
basically pushed her out of the balloon herself, by saying in her
opening remarks that she thought it was a good book but not
as good as *Portnoy*. It was Atwood's very first novel and pretty
ragged at the edges. (There is, for example, an extraordinary
silly episode where the heroine gets stuck under a bed … this
is before she goes off food, in response to the sense that she is
being consumed by her fiancé.)

This left two votes for Roth and one each for Fowles and
Greene. Kate put up a good fight for *Travels with my Aunt*
as life-affirming – though on reading this one again, I found
Greene's Catholicism seeping into bits I didn't want, the racism

uncomfortable and the knowing references to (and parodies of) his other novels a bit too self-consciously artful.

I had decided that *French Lieutenant's Woman* was brilliant. I had been assigned it by the management rather than chosen it – and had feared that it wouldn't be half as good as I remembered from first reading it as a moody adolescent (the other side of the coin from the one who tried to annoy with *Portnoy's Complaint* … no problem packing this in the satchel). In fact, it was better. Fowles seemed to me to have pulled off the nearly impossible feat of reflecting radically on the nature of our engagement with the Victorian past, and the nature of the novelist's task, while still telling a wonderful story.

However, as neither Kate nor I would give way, *Portnoy* limped home to victory.

It wasn't a popular choice with the audience, who I think ranked it (on a show of hands) on a par with the Atwood. In audience terms, the triumph was probably Kate's who had taken a good few votes from *The French Lieutenant's Woman* by the time of the final ranking. (Damn … how did I manage to lose votes … ? Too bloody academic, I guess.)

Comments

I'm with Somerset Maugham on this, who said that the way to treat the 'Book of the Moment' of his day was not to read the thing for at least three or four years … It was amazing, he said, how many 'must-reads' turned out to be 'don't-bothers' after a lapse of time.
ANNA

Being all about sex doesn't necessarily sink a work – *Y Tu Mamá También* pulls it off. (But it's hard.) A maniacal monologue can

be a masterpiece – Hamsun's *Hunger*. And misogyny can be
fascinating: *The Kreutzer Sonata*. But Roth isn't in that league.
(To give him his due: I didn't have any trouble turning the pages.
Portnoy's Complaint is an easy read.)

GABRIELLA GRUDER-PONI

Prof. Beard, You have entirely missed the point of *Portnoy's
Complaint*.

It is not about masturbation. It is, instead, a searing look
into the Jewish-ethnic-male identity circa 1960s. Any man
who's grown up in an ethnic-immigrant household in America
has his entire life story etched out in the pages of that book:
the perpetual feelings of inferiority; the smothering embrace
of insecure parents; the being torn between Old World morality
and New World sexual pleasures; the daily humiliations of not
understanding the dominant culture

ORS

Is the title of the book ambiguous? Portnoy complains / Portnoy
has a complaint = illness?

ANTHONY ALCOCK

I cannot resist praising *Solitary Sex: A Cultural History of
Masturbation* (ZONE BOOKS, 2003) by my colleague Thomas
Laqueur, which rightly links concern about masturbation with the
development of ideas of credit in the eighteenth century. And
DH Lawrence (not a figure I enjoy quoting, though he did pen
a splendid poem against the University of Nottingham and its
benefactor Mr Boot) argued that masturbation was what defined
the middle classes.

QH FLACK

Pedicabo ego vos et irrumabo: what was Catullus on about?

25 November 2009

Lucky Catullus. He has had more publicity in the last 24 hours than in the last 24 years. Whole cohorts of journalists who have never read a word of this first-century BC poet have been puzzling (with the help of Wiki usually) about what the words 'pedicabo ego vos et irrumabo' really mean.

Because these were the words written by city bigwig Mark Lowe in an email to a young woman who had asked him the meaning of 'diligite inimicos vestros'.

What it means is quite simple (though a number of family newspapers have refrained from printing a translation without a good few dashes and asterisks): 'I will ram my cock up your ass and down your throat.'

Mark Lowe's defence is that Catullus was being witty. A few journalists have half-sided with him – suggesting that this was meant as a lusty retort to the Latin she wanted him to translate. The passage, which is from St Matthew, says 'love your enemies'. No, says Catullus, bugger them.

If anyone had actually read (and thought about) the complete poem – for the offending phrase is the first and last line of Catullus Poem 16 – they would have seen a better joke and a better defence.

For it's a poem about an old conundrum: can you deduce a person's character or behaviour from what they write? Catullus addresses Furius and Aurelius (the 'queer' and the 'faggot'), who have suggested, that because he writes poems about kisses, he might be a little on the effeminate side.

Not a bit of it, says our poet. You can't tell a man from his verses. And 'pedicabo ego vos et irrumabo' for saying you can. But the joke is (or rather one of the jokes in this complicated little poem) – if you can't infer from his kiss-y verses that he is effeminate, then neither can you infer from his poetic threats of violent penetration that he is capable of that either.

Get it?

That would have been a much better defence for Mr Lowe.

First rule for undergraduates: always check where the quote actually comes from!

Comments

As JN Adams wrote in what, but for the unfortunate overtones, might be called his seminal work, *The Latin Sexual Vocabulary*, 'Catullus' "pedicabo ego uos et irrumabo" scarcely indicates a real intention on Catullus' part, but is verbal aggression.' Should we take the 'verbal aggression' as a threat? I don't think so. The verbal aggression in English for 'pedicabo' would be 'Bugger you!', but if you say that, you are not threatening to bugger the other person and, of course, a woman can say it, who would not be physically able to.

MICHAEL BULLEY

Without wanting to lower the tone too much, I think the modern English might have finally furnished a fairly exact translation for 'irrumare': 'to face-fuck'. I've certainly overheard it down the pub. The word that is, not the process.

KIRSTY MILLS

Oh my, I do lead a sheltered life!

SW FOSKA

'Arse-about-face' is probably the *mot juste* here.

TOM

I am very impressed. Mark Lowe managed in a swift move to liven up not only the debate on Catullus translation but also an otherwise dead language. He used Latin in daily context, without bothering to offer a translation, assuming that he would be perfectly understood. He must be an inspiration to our students and a shiny example to Classicists. Therefore, I was wondering if we should send him a collective congratulatory letter thanking him for his contribution.

CONSTANTINA KATSARI

I've just remembered another controversy involving Catullus 16 and I've now checked the references. The London Examination Board had prescribed, for the A level Latin exams to be taken in the summer of 1989, a selection of Catullus's poems, including poems 15, 16 and 25. Then, in March of 1989, the Board, acting on objections whose source was never revealed, declared that those three poems would not form the basis of any of the questions in the literature exam. A sad day.

MICHAEL BULLEY

Should the Rosetta Stone go back ... where?

11 December 2009

What is the best-selling postcard in the British Museum?

The last time I inquired – admittedly more than a decade ago, but was told that it was the permanent 'Number 1' – it was a rather dreary image of the Rosetta Stone. That outsold its major rivals by several thousand. If you are interested, the main postcard rivals were: various views of the Museum itself, the (also Egyptian) bronze 'Gayer Anderson' cat (displayed on the card plus or minus a real live tabby cat) and an original drawing of Beatrix Potter's *Flopsy Bunnies*.

There is no doubt that the Rosetta Stone is a major icon of the British Museum – and in fact, its postcard celebrity is backed up by its presence on best-selling umbrellas, duvet covers and mouse mats (remember them?), all especially popular, I am told, in Japan.

I was once very puzzled about all this. After all, it is a rather uninspiring lump of black basalt, inscribed at the beginning of the second century BC, recording an agreement between the Greek king of Egypt and a group of Egyptian priests, concerned, among other things, with tax breaks for the said priests. It came to London, as spoils of war in the early nineteenth century, captured from the French.

So why so charismatic?

Presumably because it was the key to decoding Egyptian hieroglyphs, as the inscription was trilingual – in hieroglyphs,

Greek and Egyptian demotic. Whether you think that the key work was done by Thomas Young (British) or Jean-François Champollion (French) depends partly on your national prejudice.

And now, again, Zahi Hawass (Secretary-General of the Supreme Council of Antiquities in Egypt) wants it 'back'? Does he have a point?

In my view, no – not at all. And I am not just talking here about the British Museum's claims to be a centre of world culture, symbolically (at least) owned by the whole world. (The current Director is very fluent and convincing on this subject.) On this Egyptian issue I feel a bit more jingoistic than usual.

For a start, let's be honest, if this boring lump of basalt has become an icon, it was because of the linguistic work of either a Brit or a Frenchman. It wasn't *born* an icon, it *became* an icon by a lot of hard academic grind (with huge 'impact' if we are going to talk HEFCE – that's 'Higher Education Funding Council for England' – talk). At that time, the state of Egypt did not exist, and 'Egyptians' had nothing to do with its decipherment. Sad but true.

If it should go back anywhere, it should be to France (as it seems pretty clear to me that, national prejudices apart, Champollion was the key figure here).

But more than that, I find myself suffering from an increasingly severe allergy to Zawi Hawass. He might once have been a good archaeologist, but he has become a nationalist media showman (complete with mad theories about famous ancient Egyptian graves, and a TV crew, plus a book signing, always at his back). He appears to have a checklist of some icons he wants 'back' to Egypt – as if they had been stolen.

I remember him on the *Today* programme a few years ago in discussion with some female descendant of Howard Carter (excavator of Tutankhamun). He was in full flow complaining about how the Brits had ripped everything off, when she politely pointed out that actually the whole Tut treasure had been left in Egypt (which did by then exist).

Today you can go and visit his fiefdom in the Antiquities Service of Egypt. It is truly amazing stuff, and no one is remotely suggesting removing it. But an awful lot in the marvellous Egyptian museum in Cairo is in a truly dreadful conservation state. (Take a look at the Fayum portraits disintegrating there.) Now the truth is that, in a global culture, we should all be paying to preserve this material for all of us, the world over, for the next few centuries. But that can only happen if Hawass stops making a media splash by demanding the Rosetta Stone and stops ignoring the much more exciting treasures crumbling on his watch.

Comments

The highlight of my visit to England in the summer of 1971 was the time I got to spend in the British Museum, and second only to the Elgin Marbles was the Rosetta Stone.

I was a newly graduated Classics major and just back from Italy and Greece, and I was once again in the presence of a piece of antiquity that I had read about since grade school. At the time I found it, no one else was around. It wasn't enclosed back then, so I double-checked to make sure I was alone, then reached out and touched it. I ran my fingertips over the hieroglyphs, the demotic text and the Greek, then read the Greek aloud, just to myself.

I went home to America a few days later, happy with that memory.

AL SCHLAF

There's a sarsen stone in our village churchyard; nobody knows its origin, but we are all ready to truckle as soon as somebody comes out of the woodwork demanding its return.

Give Stonehenge back to Wales, I say.

ANNA

Hawass is a bloviating fool.

But, that doesn't change the fact that Prof. Beard is making the classic orientalist argument here: 'WE interpreted and gave meaning to YOUR culture, therefore we reserve the right to appropriate it as we see fit.'

If you really think that the stone should stay here (and I do), you really need to offer a much better argument.

ORS

For people who want to get really close to the Rosetta Stone, there's always the charming Musée des Écritures in Champollion's home town of Figeac. Behind the museum there's a little square entirely covered by a very large replica of the stone that you can run around on. It's great fun, and would no doubt be able to accommodate an entire Egyptian department of Egyptology, with camera team.

SABINE

What to cut in universities?

13 January 2010

I went into work about 8.15 this morning, just when Michael Arthur, the chair of the Russell Group of universities, was on the *Today* programme complaining about government cuts in higher education.

He was right, of course. Compare France and Germany, whose response to the recession has been to increase university funding. (Even if that funding is more PR than real, it still says something that Sarkozy and Merkel think that more money into higher education will be a popular move.) And he didn't do badly, but he didn't do that well either. You would have thought that he would have prepared some kind of answer to the obvious question: 'So if we are not going to save money on universities, where should the savings come from?' I suppose it would have been hard for him to say what many of us think: ID cards, Trident, Afghanistan. But he might have had some clever riposte up his sleeve. In fact, he was floored.

And I didn't take too well to all that jargon about 'the knowledge economy' and 'the sector': the former is a bureaucrat's word for what I do (teaching and research), the latter a bureaucrat's word for universities. But overall for me Arthur was on the side of the angels, compared with many of the commenters on the *Guardian*'s website – who posted in response to the paper's article on university cuts (the article which had prompted the *Today* interview).

OK, some of them had some good words to say for us. But a large number were of the opinion that universities were a waste of time, that degrees could well be done in two years because we didn't bother to teach the kids anyway, and that Oxbridge dons were an especially lazy load of tossers. As one put it, there were 'plenty of people doing "useless" degrees, usually at Oxbridge with names like Classics and three 8-week terms with the final term dedicated to exams (yes that's 16 weeks per year for a degree level education and perhaps 3 tutorial hours per week)'.

I wish he (or she) could have seen my, pretty ordinary, term-time day – which went something like this:

I was at work at home at 7.30 in the morning – emailing students, about things that had come in over night. I went to the Classics Faculty at 8.15, to get some essay and lecture bibliographies together. At 10.00 I had a meeting about promotions in another faculty (I'm the internal 'external' rep) … I was back in Classics again at about 11.45 in time to see five graduate students in a row and get to my college, my other place of work, by 2.30.

After five minutes with my assistant (yes I know I am very lucky on that score …), who had done some industrial quantities of xeroxing, I saw each of the Newnham Classics third-years for 15 minutes, to discuss their work schedule for the term (cutting it fine, and I got behind, but they are all coming to my home on Sunday evening, when the loose ends can be picked up). After that I saw groups of first- and second-years, a second-year historian from another college who will be taking ancient history with me this term, and a third-year whose dissertation I'm supervising … then a graduate I hadn't met before, who is going to be doing some work on Jane Harrison.

I got home by about 7.00. The husband had done supper, so that I could start going through draft exam papers. I'm an exam board chair, and I needed to read over all the papers submitted for an examiners meeting tomorrow, looking for errors, duplications, typos etc. That took until 12.30 ... which I reckon is a 17-hour day, minus a half-hour for supper.

The knowledge economy on overtime.

So where might we save money in 'the sector'? Well, the husband had a bright idea during our brief supper. Given these times of stringency, shouldn't we be abolishing the REF? (That's the Research Excellence Framework for those of you not in the 'sector'.) It isn't going to tell us anything we didn't know anyway ... and it must cost millions. At least enough to save a few hard-working academics and departments from the axe. In other walks of life, this would be called pruning the bureaucrats and channelling resources to the front line (i.e., the teachers ...).

Comments

I think part of the problem is the fetish for working hard. I'd say that, in a country like Britain at least, society would be better if people did less and did it more slowly. The cabbages are going to grow at the same rate.

MICHAEL BULLEY

I think your daily diary may play into the hands of the nay-sayers, because you don't address the fact that this sort of day is only typical of less than half your year. One of the politicians could make the same sort of claim of long days, but we don't therefore claim they are doing a good job ...

I am worried about the lack of lunch!

SEBASTIAN RAHTZ

'More money' spent on German universities means 'finally some'.

ANTHONY ALCOCK

The eighteenth-century Dean Gaisford of Christ Church, Oxford, is to be recommended. He propounded a philosophy of 'systematic lethargy'. There's a lot to be said for that. He also encouraged the study of Greek because 'it not infrequently leads to positions of considerable emolument' – though he probably had in mind the Church of England rather than the more general economy.

PAUL POTTS

I wonder if the need to justify our contribution based on our busy SCHEDULES means the bureaucrats are clearly winning and learning no longer speaks for itself. I would like to see A Don's Day which talks more about the lessons which were imparted, the mysteries that were revealed and the passions that were awakened.

ROGER DAVIS

Are you at risk of plagiarism?

14 February 2010

On Friday evening I gave a Darwin Lecture in Cambridge in
a series on the theme of 'Risk'. These lectures – which happen
every Friday in Lent term – have been going for 25 years now
and have become something of a Cambridge institution, with a
new theme each year (Serendipity, Survival, Identity, Evidence
…), and a vast audience. I was in the Lady Mitchell Hall, which
takes 500, and then there was a video link to an overflow hall.

My theme was 'Risk and the Humanities', and most of the
lecture was actually about how the ancient Greeks and Romans
approached and faced danger – and how and why the ancients
didn't have a 'risk agenda' anything like our own. But in the
last five minutes I allowed myself a bit of a rant about how that
risk agenda, in the modern sense, had distorted research and
teaching in the humanities now.

Grant awarding bodies like the AHRC (Arts & Humanities
Research Council) are so risk-averse, that when you apply for
money they make you specify exactly what your outcomes
are going to be, and exactly what your timetable of research
is going to be. Not only is this a complete misrepresentation
of how humanities research is carried out (you don't know
how long it is going to take you to read a book – it all depends
how interesting you make it), but it also encourages us all to
dishonesty. For the only way sensibly to be able to conform
to the AHRC guidelines is to apply for money for research
you've already done … that's the dream ticket for risk aversion.
There's no problem with the outcomes and you use the

research time they pay for to get on with the next project ... then in due course you apply for more money to fund that (even though you've already done it).

After the lecture people told me that was regular practice in lab-based sciences.

But the other poisonous thing about the risk agenda in universities is that it has started to cast risk in the Chernobyl mode – I mean, as a nasty thing that you can be a victim of, rather than something over which you have responsibility and control yourself.

Take plagiarism: it's ceasing to be the crime of 'cheating' and is becoming an appalling academic disaster that can happen to you unawares, without you even knowing you have done it.

If you don't believe me, check out the University of East Anglia, Anti-Plagiarism quiz: 'Are you at risk of plagiarism?'

Naively I thought at first that this must mean 'Are you at risk of *being* plagiarised?' But no, it means 'Are you are risk of being a plagiariser?' And its 13 questions get over a few key facts on the modern plagiarism/risk agenda. Yes, it is possible to plagiarise without realising that you have. And no, fear of plagiarism should not stop you talking to fellow students about your work, so long as you are sensible. Etc.

It all made plagiarism sound like a nasty disease you might pick up without knowing, but one that shouldn't stop ordinary social contact (so long as you don't share a toothbrush or anything silly like that).

And after all, as one of my colleagues pointed out, 'plagiarism' actually sounds like a disease; 'cheating' doesn't.

Comments

I don't think interpreting 'Are you at risk of plagiarism?' as 'Are
you at risk of being plagiarised?' is naive. That's what it should
mean. For UEA to have intended it to mean 'How likely is it that
you might unwittingly commit plagiarism?' is like using 'Are you at
risk of execution?' to mean 'Might you absent-mindedly execute
someone?'

MICHAEL BULLEY

I deal with plagiarising students all the time. The vast majority of
them know they're cheating, those that don't have missed lectures
and tutorials in 1st year, where we explain why it is wrong, and
for them we have a system which starts with a written warning for
first offenders so they get a chance to mend their ways. Hardly an
'appalling academic disaster', more a considered response to a real
and serious problem in today's universities.

ROB KNELL

The insurance industry ought to be getting in on this.

PL

In the worlds of ideas and culture (to name a few), copywrong and
patents (intellectual property) are far, far more destructive than
borrowing humanity's collective creations and developing them.
Emulation, progress, prosperity – they're all bound and gagged
and chained upside down in inaccessible dungeons. ('Inaccessible'
presumably meaning you can't access the outside, in NewSpeak.)

If a student can present commonplaces better than the last documented presenter then good on her! If not, tough titty and down go his grades.

XJY

Is the fear of being accused of plagiarism why so many authors of academic books and journal articles list, in the bibliography, a set of works it would take ten lifetimes to read?

MICHAEL BULLEY

That might be one reason for the monster bibliographies you see in some academic books. Two other, more obvious, ones are: to thicken the product so it can be sold for more and to back-scratch colleagues who have their own books to flog and will back-scratch (cite) you in return. Typical vices of a command economy.

PL

In *Ghost Train to the Eastern Star*, Paul Theroux quotes Pedro Almodóvar as saying: 'Anything that is not autobiography is plagiarism.'

ROSEMARY MEECHAN

Plagiarism is considered a fine way of getting A-level grades. We were told 'If you can remember what we've said about this text, say it in the exam' as the first rule. Then for bonus points, 'if you can remember who said it first, give their name'. According to people I know doing A levels now, it hasn't changed much, hence, poor conscientious students writing that 'Teacher X says that hubris is the cause of the hero's downfall'. Because obviously, Teacher X said it first.

LUCY

In my experience, students are right to be petrified. A friend of mine from university (*c.* ten years ago) committed a minor error: citing a lecturer in an essay rather than the original work that the lecturer had been discussing. Afterwards, she felt uneasy about her actions, so she told the lecturer what she'd done. The lecturer reported her to the undergraduate judicial board – a panel of administrator-selected undergrads. Keen to prove their toughness on 'plagiarists' in the wake of a major campus scandal, the board suspended – I guess the Oxbridge term would be 'sent down' – my friend for an entire term.

MARGARET

What about jazz musicians? When we improvise, the music comes from inside somewhere, without conscious thought, but we are influenced by all the music we ever heard.

OURSALLY

I came into this world with nothing, and all I know has been learned from others and from books. I have been reading for 65 years, and hardly bother to read a book's title or the name of the author, all soon forgotten as the years pass.   Plagiarism seems a device of university professors to protect their interests or frighten their students.

BRIAN LEWIS

How many references do you write in a week?

19 February 2010

This is a little moan about writing references. But let me make one thing clear right at the beginning: evaluating students, ex-students and colleagues is an important part of my job; I'm not complaining about being asked to do it (so no need to feel remotely guilty about asking me) – I'm complaining about the cumbersome, inefficient and sometimes downright obstructive infrastructure.

Let's get the scale of the problem. Although the number goes down at other times of the year, between October and the end of February (the peak postgraduate, milk-round and research fellowship recruiting season), I write on average something like 10–12 references a week; in January this year it was more like 15–16. The time it takes to write and process each one varies – from say an hour and a half if you are writing something from scratch (and it would be longer for a complicated and unusual job) to 15 minutes for something simple for a student whose reference you already have on your computer (whoops, is that or is it not against the Data Protection Act?)

Overall then, it is an average of about 30 minutes a reference, or 8 hours a week at peak times.

Now in the old days when I did fewer (this is a task that naturally gets bigger as you get older and have more ex-students wanting jobs, chairs, research leave, promotion), the system was a lot more homogeneous. Before email, you would get a written request from the student asking if you would mind them using your name, and you would then get a letter from the employer or the college or department asking you to send it. You would pile these up on your desk and work through them one by one. For even the most untidy or scatty reference writer, it was hard to forget them or mislay one.

Normally, when you had sent the reference off, you got a thank-you letter from the potential employer. I remember that when Henry Chadwick was Master of Peterhouse he used to send beautifully handwritten thank-you cards (which made you feel good, and made you take care the next time).

It isn't like that now. In fact it's a nightmare.

For a start, students email you to ask if you will do it – and as often as not you are supposed just to send the thing off, without any other request from the employer or university. Even if your email inbox is in a lot neater state than mine, the request can easily disappear among all the opened messages and you simply forget about it (not like when it was sitting there looking at you on your *real* desktop). I now say to people who want me to write for them that it is *their* responsibility to make sure that I have done it. But I still panic in the middle of the night that I have forgotten one – and sometimes I have.

The next problem is that many educational institutions now have some version of on-line reference submission. Just occasionally this works a treat. You get a password, it opens up into a clear, easy to use form, you get an acknowledgement when you have finished – and on the best systems the computer sends you a reminder a few days before the deadline.

But not often. Sometimes the password doesn't work. Sometimes the system is 'down'. Then all you can do is send frantic emails to whatever contact address the system allows you to have. It took me several days to submit a reference to the British Academy a few months ago – and I only managed it after someone in their office had pointed out that the colon in front of the password I had been sent was actually part of the password (not, as I had assumed, just the colon in front of it). It's all a race against time too. Because if you're late they disable your password and, without a tearful series of begging emails, and a few fibs about having been ill, they won't enable it again.

Sometimes the whole electronic system just seems jinxed (or what they call in the trade 'compatibility problem with your Mac'). After Christmas I was trying to fill in a Cambridge reference form which the student had sent me by email, and then print it out so that it could be sent, as instructed, in an envelope. I could fill the damn thing in OK, but when it came to printing it out, it simply deleted all I had written. Several times over. That's irritating enough when you are just doing one; when you have another ten in the queue by tomorrow, it makes you cry.

Not that the modern *non*-computerised system is any better. No longer do you often send it off directly to the university concerned. No, that means that they have to employ someone to match up your reference with the student's application. To save themselves money and to maximise your irritation, many departments now have feeble, barely secure systems where you hand the reference back to the student in an envelope, signed across the seal and then covered with Sellotape. It's hardly enough to keep an enterprising applicant with a kettle from finding out what you've written … and the times I've been doing it at home and failed to find any Sellotape are too many now to count.

Nor is there much Chadwick-style personal gratitude on display. The best you can hope for is the automatic computer message 'Thank you very much for submitting your reference. It will be most helpful to the college in the selection process.' You are more likely simply to read on the form: 'As the college receives so many applications, it is impossible to acknowledge individual references.' (Well, actually, I bet it took the well-trained Chadwick several evenings to write all his thank-you cards.) But the ones I really can't stand come from rather brash HR departments. They don't just say, 'Sorry we can't acknowledge', but they impose an impossible timetable and a measure of blackmail too. Typical would be an email on Monday lunchtime, saying they have just short-listed Dr X and get your reference in by Thursday, otherwise Dr X's chances of the job will be seriously diminished.

But the planet that HR departments inhabit is, as we know, not the same as ours.

Comments

This says everything I feel about the worst elements of the 'internet age'. Mercifully, when I had to write references I did just that and talked to the one requesting the reference in person. I remember Henry Chadwick very well when he was Dean of Queens'. Delightful, kind, a brilliant mind and amusingly pedantic: any 'Good morning' wished to him at one minute past midday resulted in his reaching into his pocket for his watch and, after a confirmatory glance, 'Good afternoon!' in response.
RICHARDH

Dear Mary I'm tempted to guess
Of the reference/s you address

There is some certain law
As you write more and more
The jobs they concern all get less.

(/ is my feeble attempt at an accent indicating that the word, for reasons of stress, is pronounced referensez)

QH FLACK

Has anybody actually delayed so long in writing a reference that the student in question most probably didn't get the job? I was once asked to send a reference for a Modern Languages student so awful that I wouldn't have employed her as a cleaner. While I delayed and dithered and wondered how to praise her with least faint damn, the deadline passed …

ROSEMARY MEECHAN

Perhaps Mary should be aware that one has the right to see references written about oneself, so the pseudo-security has little effect.

Personally, I use references to confirm that the person is not actually lying when they say they studied Coptic. Beyond that, I seldom find them useful as a discriminator between candidates. About as much use as that bit on the application form where they list 'reading, playing computer games, and travelling' as their interests.

SEBASTIAN RAHTZ

And then there's the related problem of refereeing conference and journal papers. In the old days that, too, was a gift economy: people helped each other. You referee this paper for my journal: I'll be on the jury of your student's thesis. Now that's gone, and

it's all just spam: endless requests for reports on papers in which
I've no interest. So I hit the delete button. So does everyone else,
and the volume of requests keeps on growing as the robots get
more desperate. Where does it end? Shall we see a paper in ten
years time entitled 'The Peer Review System – Tragic Loss or Good
Riddance?'

ROSS ANDERSON

'It's hardly enough to keep an enterprising applicant with a kettle
from finding out what you've written …'

   How mysteriously interesting! A kettle! Could you be more
explicit as to what the process actually entails … ?

CLEM

Clem – the old technique of STEAMING a letter open!

MARY BEARD

My tutor at Girton was a Classicist. She did her best with the small
crowd of engineers. Since my industrial sponsor built objects
normally painted olive-green, they needed to check up on my
activities to see if I had become a Communist spy – not unusual at
Cambridge in those days. So they wrote a letter, and she called me
to her office and I had to tell her what to write: 'Did you join the
Communist Party? Well, you would hardly tell me if you had. Did
you have homosexual relationships? An impertinent question!'
And so on. She did put the right answers, though, good of her, the
old dear.

OURSALLY

OK, Henry Chadwick. I was around when he was as Dean of
Christ Church. He looked every inch the part, was a serial

embarrassment. He once insisted that an undergraduate who had been reported as having a girl (yes!) in his rooms overnight be sent down on the grounds that the College – no, the House – was religious property and could not allow that sort of thing, whatever happened elsewhere.

Chadwick was clearly living in some neglected corner of the nineteenth century. If only Trollope were still writing.

PAUL POTTS

It's not what you know, it's what you're known for … and – worth noting – it's not an individual thing. Most people sharing a set of views will have the same criteria by which they judge people. The exceptions – a Chadwick, say – are sapphires in a cesspool, or pearls in a pigsty.

XJY

How to lose an election – the Roman (or Nicholas Winterton) way

22 February 2010

Some time in the second century BC, a member of the aristocratic Scipio family lost an election. Standing for the office of *aedile*, he had been eagerly canvassing the people – and happened to shake the hands of a peasant. Now the peasant's hands were horny, from all his tough agricultural labour and Scipio – being an effete toff – was not used to the feel. 'Wot,' he said (as a joke?), 'do you walk on these?'

Now Rome may not have been a radical democracy, but the Roman people didn't put up with toffs insulting the honest labouring poor, and they took their revenge. Scipio lost the election. That, at least is the story handed down by the early imperial writer Valerius Maximus in a section of his *Memorable Deeds and Sayings* devoted to people who lost elections. (The Latin text is Book 7, 5, 2.)

It's not the kind of revenge that the British electorate will get to take on Nicholas Winterton for his aspersions on those of us who usually travel in Standard Class on the trains. He is standing down from parliament anyway.

(Actually, in fairness to Winterton, at many hours of the day it is totally impossible to work in Standard Class between Cambridge and London – you would be lucky to get a seat, and opening a laptop would be impossible. Your blogger has occasionally been known to shell out for First Class, when she has been desperate to get something done.)

All in all, it's hard not to feel a bit envious of Roman face-to-face politics – compared with what we shall get in May or whenever.

It's not just the trained-monkey, American-style spectacle of the televised debate that looks set to remove yet more real argument out of the electoral process. The papers have been full of the Labour Party's clever wheezes in using social networking etc. to get to us voters. What this appears to mean is that we will be bombarded with text messages on our mobiles, automated phone messages and whatever they can possibly get on Facebook or Twitter.

Douglas Alexander boasted last week of a new phase of 'peer-to peer communication', saying that 'Labour had made 400,000 voter contacts in marginal seats since the start of the year, using software that allows members to set up phone banks in their own homes and build a relationship with them.' I hope you don't live in a marginal seat. Because if you do, what this really means is that you will be bombarded with calls connected to a taped message urging you to vote Labour … which will go on regardless, whether you tell them to piss off or not. Forget the 'relationship'. When I was in Berkeley, during the last presidential election, I was renting a house from a registered Democrat – and the automated democrats were on to him about 20 times a day.

What happened to doorstepping? And what happened to going down to your local forum, shaking the candidate's hand and seeing what you think of him (or her)?

Come back, Scipio, you're forgiven.

Comments

If my MP were reading confidential correspondence on the train, I would certainly hope he were doing so at his own table in First Class.

GEOFFREY WALKER

As for Mr Winterton, I think that his precise mistake was this. There are people in the market economy who get to travel First Class, because their employers have decided that it is worth it, allowing them to get more done on the train. Employers are entitled to take decisions like that, because they are subject to the discipline of the market: if they are too extravagant, they go bust. Mr W decided that it would be good value to send himself First Class, but there is no independent (market) check on the accuracy of his evaluation of his own time and productivity.

RICHARD BARON

Lecturers – beware germs

16 March 2010

I have moaned before about pointless health and safety notices (like the one urging drunks to take care on the station platform – for those drunks compos mentis enough to stop and read the notice). But the USA sometimes presents even more aggressive examples of the nanny state.

I have just had a great time in Madison, but was a bit surprised to find one of those containers of hygienising 'wipes' on the podium in the lecture room. I wasn't sure exactly what the point was. Was I supposed to sterilise my own hands so that I didn't pollute the lecturing control panel? Or was I supposed to use them to wipe the microphone and the switches and computer connections etc., in case there were some threatening germs still lurking from the previous user?

It reminded me of those US supermarkets where they give you an antiseptic wipe to clean the handle of the trolley with (or your own hands?) before you load it up with your food ... and indeed of all those women whom I found in Berkeley used their feet to flush the loo, and assumed that was normal.

I guess I am counter-suggestible in the hygiene department, as in others ... but when I see a notice in a loo urging me to wash my hands to prevent the outbreak of whatever plague we are currently fighting, I am *less* likely to do it than if there is no warning notice at all, and I can treat myself as a responsible individual who can and will make responsible decisions.

I was reflecting on this as I waited at Madison airport, following a visit to the Ladies, which was more than usually kitted out with

WITH THE WINTER
VOMITING VIRUS
GOING AROUND,
PLEASE WASH YOUR
HANDS PROPERLY.

hygiene notices. In fact, I was wondering if those wartime posters about 'Careless talk costing lives' would have made me more or less likely to blab to the handsome stranger about the current location of all the soldiers I knew, or the latest developments at Bletchley Park ... when, even worse, a loud announcement was made over the airport tannoy to all and sundry.

Yes, it was urging all passengers to wash their hands carefully and to sneeze, if they must, into a tissue.

At least we can be thankful that the States has so far resisted the British obsession with CCTV cameras, else they would no doubt be installed in loos just to make sure that no hand was left unscrubbed.

Comments

Some emails I now receive from offices have an automatic closing message: 'Think of the environment – do you need to print this email?' My instant reaction is always, 'Why yes, now you mention it, I should print it for my records.'

ALEX

If we stop spreading germs, our immune systems will be weakened and we will fall prey, with horrific results, to the first unusual epidemic. So the nanny state has got it wrong as always.

THELEASTER

It is certainly interesting to note different practices currently and through time in things that are marginally to do with hygiene (like the foot-flushers of Berkeley). In southern Europe you will see men in the open air (men, rather than women) closing one nostril and jet-propelling the contents of the other on to the ground (I've never acquired the knack myself). Many northern Europeans find that revolting, while many southern Europeans are equally revolted by the sight of someone putting their snot into a cloth handkerchief and then putting the handkerchief into their pocket.

MICHAEL BULLEY

Here in Sweden they want you to sneeze in the crook of your arm. But at the office we have a culture of explosive sneezing to brighten everyone's day and show our lungs are in good shape.

XJY

I recently attended a negotiating session with (or I should say against) some HR types. We shook hands cordially and customarily. The HR types promptly sanitised their hands but did not pass the container over to our side of the table. Never felt so insulted in my life.

PAT CHANDLER

Lavatory etiquette's quite a to-do.
How should you flush when you're done in the loo?
Some push the handle while still on the seat
And the women of Berkeley all flush with their feet!

MICHAEL BULLEY

Why 'good practice' can ruin good practice

6 April 2010

When I was a graduate student, things were different. I didn't have to fill in many forms – in fact, I think I just applied for a British Academy grant (as it then was) to work on a PhD in nothing more than 'Roman history'. I wasn't given a code of practice. If I wanted to learn something (like a new language), I went off and did it; I didn't demand a specially targeted Faculty class in it ('Turkish for Roman historians', or whatever).

My supervisor didn't bother me too much (though he did give me a few big kicks towards the end). Whenever I wanted to see him, I sent him a note (pre-email) and he would have me round, and I would stay for as long as it took to go over my work or my problems. If I wanted to talk to one of the other senior Faculty members, I would catch them after a seminar or in the library, and we would have coffee or (more often) a drink.

I am sure that this laid-back, unregulated system let some students down. (We all heard stories/urban myths about PhD students who had not seen their supervisors in 12 months.) But it worked wonderfully for me and for many of my friends – and probably much better than what we now offer to our graduates.

Now, if students want funding, they have to explain what they will discover before they start. (The best applications are, as most of us suspect, written by the supervisor.) When they arrive on their course, they are given codes of practice up to their ears: they know how often they should meet their supervisors, they have regular reviews with other members of the Faculty, they have a secondary supervisor (in case their first one isn't good enough), and they even have log books in which they can register their contact with their supervisor (in which I fear a jolly good, intellectually productive, discussion in the pub doesn't quite count – how wrong is that?).

All these initiatives were, I am sure, very well intentioned. They were intended to make sure that PhD students didn't go for 12 months without seeing their supervisors, or didn't take seven years to finish their theses or, worse still, didn't fail at the end of the process. But I do wonder if the baby hasn't been thrown out with the bath water. To put it another way, despite (or because of) our good intentions, I suspect that most graduate students now have a worse 'learning experience' than we did – at a time before we knew what a 'learning experience' was.

The point is that I am now so busy with supervising, being a secondary supervisor interviewing applicants for graduate funding, doing first-, second- and third-year reviews that I am simply not available any more to meet a graduate student for coffee after half a morning in the library. So I go through the tick-box routines, but don't any longer have the time to chill out with a student, doing what I am best at (and what my own teachers were best at) – which is just talking about the ancient world.

And it isn't only a question of graduate students. Similar changes have happened in my relations with my colleagues and my undergraduates. When I started my lectureship at Cambridge (in 1984), we used often to go to each other's

lectures. It wasn't to rate them, but to learn – yet of course, if
you were just starting out, it was really useful to talk to your
older colleagues about what you (or they) had said. That useful
practice has stopped, because we are all too busy going to the
lectures of those we are officially 'mentoring' (tiptoeing around
all the awkward issues, not wanting to come to a lecture if
the lecturer might not be entirely happy, and then having an
embarrassing and almost worthless feedback session). And
we hardly ever have time to read each other's work, which was
always one of the best things, the intellectual advantages, of
being in Cambridge.

As for the undergraduates, I remember that when I was a
student, supervisions went on as long as there was something
interesting to say. That was the case too when I started
teaching at Cambridge. Now I only rarely have a supervision
that lasts more than an hour and a quarter. Why? Because my
time is taken up promoting 'good practice' and transparency.
So now our students have access to all kinds of (true but
unhelpful) documents on what kind of transferable skills they
may gain from a Classics degree, or what distinguishes a first-
class degree from a 2.1. But they have less of my time, because
I am writing this stuff, as well as being a supervisor, secondary
supervisor, mentor, appraiser, whatever …

One day, I hope, someone will look back on the way we
spend all our time on process and paper trails (rather than
doing the job and changing people's minds), and they will
wonder where, when or why we forgot what we were really
about.

Comments

At least the human subjects in Classics normally have the good grace to be dead. Imagine having to jump through all the ethics committee good practice procedures too …

HELEN

But who is it who's telling you to do this? How many academics are there in Cambridge who are grumbling as you are? Why don't you do something about it?

You are all intelligent people and could presumably write down briefly how the system should work. You could address the problems you mention that were present before but still get that baby back in the bath. When people like you meekly go along with such nonsense, it makes everyone's life harder because 'they' continue to impose their petty rules and regulations. For goodness sake, get some backbone and stand up to them.

JULIAN GALL

Julian: When you sign off your soul to Mephistopheles, he wins. He's got the enforcers on his side. He puts the food on your table. Nothing 'meek' about this – Faust wasn't meek. He just signed the wrong contract. And back in the '50s and '60s university life (in Britain) had academic freedom, tenure, optimism and excitement. Helen of Troy with a brain (girls – find your own equivalent :-)

XJY

I've said this before, but I can't see what's wrong with having to describe the content and purpose of your pedagogy. People who sell fried chicken can do this – tell you what it is they are purveying and why you might want to buy it. Why is this apparently beneath the dignity of self-proclaimed 'intelligent' people?

SW FOSKA

The one advantage of being Jewish in occupied France was that one did not have the option of collaboration.

HOGWEED

I suppose when comparing a system that is average for ten students, or brilliant for nine students and appalling and unfair for the tenth, the second system is going to seem better. Unless you were the tenth student …

KEIR FINLOW-BATES

And the prize for the worst manifesto goes to ...

15 April 2010

I spent a rather gloomy day yesterday reading the various party election manifestos. I admit that this was not in the cause of my own political development, but because I was due on the *Today* programme this morning to sound off about them, and about the 'Great Debate' between the party leaders coming up on television.

Honestly, I thought that there was not much to choose between the three main parties in this respect, though Labour and Tory were worse than Lib Dems by a short head. It wasn't just the graphics – though quite where both of the big two had found their left-over Eastern bloc propagandists, heaven knows. The Tory 'people power' illustration really did have the tractor factory feel to it – and the fact that it was indeed an advert for the *Tory* party is just one hint at the ideological emptiness that you will find if you read these documents.

As I blurted on the radio, the worst thing about these documents is their oozing platitudes. Whoever has written them has not grasped the point that political messages only count as interesting and engaging and worth bothering with if the opposite point of view could conceivably be held – if, that is, there is something to argue about. The mainstream parties give us almost nothing that most of the human race could possibly object to. 'A future fair for all' (Labour)? Sure, but the country isn't actually teeming with people who are demanding

a less fair future. 'Children should be allowed to grow up at
their own pace' (Tories)? Is anyone seriously advocating the
opposite? 'As Conservatives, we trust people'? Unlike who … ?

Often different parties actually come out with almost
exactly the same platitudes. 'Get better politics for less' (Lib
Dem) or 'Good government costs less with the Conservatives'
– in this case not only vacuous but untrue as well.

Partly, you get the impression that they are all so keen not
to offend anyone that they resort to anything bland. Partly it's
the simple absence of ideology again. (Another nice example,
the Labour Manifesto includes enthusiastic words on 'Creating
a shareholding society' – admittedly on the John Lewis model.)
Oh – and don't mention the war. There is plenty of stuff about
military equipment and hospitals, and a couple of pics of
soldiers fraternising with natives (in the Tory manifesto, with
a football). But not a word about whether we should be in
Afghanistan or not. As the husband remarked, 'People Power'
clearly doesn't extend to the 'people' of Afghanistan.

It is perhaps predictable that those furthest from any
possibility of being in government (or even winning a seat)
had the freshest approaches. After the blandness of the big
three, it was a positive relief to turn to the Communist Party.
The policies are probably barking, but I loved the front cover,
which blazons 'Britain for the People not the Bankers. Make
the Fat Cats Pay' (The 'people' may smack of the Tories, but
'Fat Cats' gives it away.) Some ideology at last.

So, which was the very worst? Well, in a very close race,
between the big three, it has to be the Labour version. Two
particular sins make it slightly worse than the others. I can't
stand the 'I love Britain' line from Gordon Brown in his
introduction (as if everyone else didn't … ?). But worse, just
before a paean of praise to the DNA database, we read 'We

are proud of our record on civil liberties'. Now either that is a whoppa – or it is self-delusion. Either way, it wins them the wooden spoon.

But anyway, I got my come-uppance for self-promotion and a few minutes of fame on the radio. One of my lines on the TV debate (about how the poor guys must have been up all night having their eyebrows plucked and learning their spontaneous jokes) was taken on to a BBC 'quotes of the day'. But sadly I wasn't. It said Mary Beard is an 'American historian and women's rights campaigner'. Shit – the wrong Mary Beard. The more famous one died in 1958, when I was three.

Comments

I am comforted by the lack of ideology. The idea that one party might impose its vision of society on all of us, including the many who disagree, or might even seek to do so, horrifies me. The real honesty challenge for politicians who lack ideology is to say so.
RICHARD BARON

One thing I like spotting in manifestos is the redundant guarantee, named for those manufacturers' guarantees that make a great fuss about granting you, as a favour, rights which are already enshrined in law. ('We will replace faulty parts free of charge for up to a year!')

My sitting MP (Tory) has a line on his manifesto which boasts to me that this leaflet has been delivered by volunteers 'at no cost to the taxpayer'. A claim which I sincerely trust is true, because if he has attempted to charge the taxpayer for his campaign expenses, he is in big trouble.
ANNA

If you want ideology, you could try the Labour Education
spokesman's doctrinaire asseveration that learning Latin is a Bad
Thing.

OLIVER NICHOLSON

Wasn't it Quintus Cicero who told his brother to never promise
anything concrete and never commit to a strong idea when on
electoral campaign?

Although I'm sure most politicians today won't have read the
Commentariolum Petitionis (none in my country), they seem to
follow some of its advice quite closely.

GI

Ten dotty (well-meaning?) ideas from the party election manifestos

29 April 2010

After a serious study of the main party manifestos, let me reveal some of the dottier ideas that have got by the party committees and into their official promises. How on earth, one wonders, do these things get the nod … ? Have you noticed them?

1. Establish a new prize for engineering.
This is a Tory idea (to 'make Britain the leading hi-tech exporter in Europe') … may not be so bad an idea, but *in the manifesto*? (No prize for Classics, I note!)

2. Create a specialist Mandarin teacher training qualification, so that many more primary schools have access to a qualified primary teacher able to teach Mandarin.
So offers the Labour party. A worthy aim … but when we can't teach French effectively? And where are these Mandarin teachers coming from?

3. Control bullying, including homophobic bullying.
Another virtuous aim (this time from the Lib Dems), but is this an appropriate manifesto commitment? I mean, how are they going to do this?

4. Launch an annual Big Society Day.
Another holiday, on which 'to celebrate the work of
neighbourhood groups' … and, presumably the work of the
middle-class mums and dads who plan to set up their own
schools. A Tory idea, needless to say.

5. The right to cancer test results within one week.
A Labour PR move. Well, who could not want speedy cancer
tests? But another target? And how easy is it for the pushy
middle class to manipulate? Next time I think I need an X-ray
for my stiff knee, I guess I persuade my GP to say 'suspected
carcinoma.'

6. Establish a free on-line database of exam papers and marking schemes – for GCSE and A/AS.
A Tory bright idea, but so far as I know, you can get this
information free already.

7. Make Network Rail refund a third of your ticket price if you have to take a rail replacement bus service.
Nice idea. Whatever Lib Dem thought this up must have lived
in Cambridge, where Network Rail regularly works on both
lines to London simultaneously. But for a party trying to cut
red tape etc. What do they think the cost of this will be?

8. Ensure that the 2013 Rugby League and 2015 Rugby Union World Cups are successful.
Ensure that we win? Or what do the Tories actually mean on
this one?

9. All relevant agencies – not just neighbourhood police teams – will hold monthly public meetings to hear people's concerns (on Anti Social Behaviour – or ASB, as the Labour party now calls it).
Well it could be useful. But as a Labour manifesto commitment??

10.Tackle the gender gap at all levels of scientific study and research to help increase the supply of scientists.
Well I'm all for this one, Lib Dems … but many of us have been working on it for years. So exactly *how* are they going to tackle it?

There's plenty more where they came from.

Comments

I am curious as to why everyone has suddenly got obsessed with Mandarin, and how if only it was available we could turn out millions of happy Mandarin speakers. Have they any idea how hard Mandarin is to learn? (I tried when I was living in China, and I didn't get very far.) And, of course, this will be all about learning to speak to Chinese businessmen, and there will be no conception of enabling people to read *Romance of the Three Kingdoms* in the original.

TONY KEEN

I find it hard to treat the phrase 'coming from' seriously, because of its use in sentences like 'I know where you're coming from.' There's a great story that some young American actor in the same play as Sir John Gielgud, wanting to pick the great man's brains, asked

him, 'Sir Gielgud, in this scene, where am I coming from exactly?'
Sir John replied, 'From the wings, dear boy, the wings.'

MICHAEL BULLEY

My partner learned Mandarin in primary school. The sole residue
of that particular piece of education is that he can sing a rather
sweet children's song about numbers and suddenly spotting
a friend. Somehow, I don't see this ability as making a strong
contribution to the UK's economic output.

LIZ

Do we need bad teachers?

12 July 2010

The retiring Chair of Ofsted (the 'Office for Standards in Education'), Zenna Atkins, has got herself into trouble (and no doubt been misquoted) in saying that it might be good for kids to learn to cope with the occasional bad teacher. Even if she is misquoted, I am with her. The idea that public services can be free from human frailty is surely bonkers. We all need to learn how to recognise and deal with a teacher/policeman/ tax-inspector/doctor we don't entirely trust – just as we learn how to deal with a private business that does not give us what we asked for. The appalling encroachment of (illusory) tick-box competence is something we need to resist; we are always going to have to deal with people who are below par (that's the definition of 'par', after all).

But the big question is not 'What do you do with bad teachers?' but 'How do you know who a bad teacher is?'

When I was an undergraduate, I was very fierce about what I considered bad lectures. In fact, a good friend of mine on one occasion went up to the then Professor of Greek (one Professor K***) and told him publicly that his lectures were a disgrace to the university. The truth is that they both were and weren't, but my friend's fully frontal confrontation was a much more effective way of raising the issue than pouring her heart out in an anonymous questionnaire.

But when I was a student activist in the 1970s, I got a shock.

We activists decided to run the first ever (I think) Classics Faculty lecture questionnaire, hoping to out the malefactors, the dull, the unconscientious (the Professor of Greek among them). The result was not what we had expected. Sure, our view on who the best and worst were got broad confirmation, but there wasn't one lecturer who was not rated tops by somebody. Unless you took the view that minority tastes were not to be catered for, then you could really not pillory anyone at all (although you might want to nudge a few of them in a slightly more popular direction).

Having done the lecturing game myself now for 30 years or more, I think that there is an even bigger problem. It is how and *when* you judge whether teaching has been a success. It is all well and good to correlate people's lectures and supervisions with final degree results. But that can't be the be-all and end-all. Because getting a first or a 2.1 isn't in the end what really matters; it's what you do with the degree next – 5, 10, 20, 30 years down the road. And of course some of our most impressive citizens got 2.2s years ago, and they have been inspired no doubt in the long term by what might have seemed at the time to be, at best, inefficient teaching.

The trouble about assessing bad teaching is that some of what you think is bad aged 21 turns out to be the most influential and inspirational when you look back aged 41 – even Professor K***'s.

Comments

No, a bad teacher is a bad teacher and time does not alter the fact. Over the decades there is no way I can warm to the school teacher who dictated incomprehensible notes on Palmerston and Gladstone to be learned by heart, or to the Cambridge law lecturer who just read out sections of the recommended text book (Buckland) in the most dreary voice imaginable. We coped with the history teacher by playing his game or going through the motions, and with the law lecturer by simply staying away, so we did learn something about adaptation and survival … and how not to be bad teachers ourselves.

BOB

Mary's witty bit on the meaning of par is what idiomatic, spontaneous English is all about, even for those who dislike golf. As to lectures, many people must have been encouraged by Leavis's remark that if students wanted what they got from most lectures, they could go to the books it came from.

PETER WOOD

I'm going to have to confess that I don't see what 'Mary's witty bit on the meaning of par' is. Can you explain? I hope there's not a confusion here between par and average, as that's the sort of tangle Ofsted itself has often got caught up in.

MICHAEL BULLEY

Anthony Powell said that in learning to be a writer he profited more from bad authors, whose vices he could recognise and learn to avoid, than from good ones, whose virtues were often inimitable. Might there be some application of this via negativa to the teacher question?

PL

Civilian casualties, leaks and the ancient view

26 July 2010

By and large, Greek and Roman military command had it relatively easy when it came to leaks, civilian casualties and the PR side of warfare. To put it at its crudest, the imperial Roman legions would go off to conquer some bit of foreign territory, they would do it any way they could and come back home and boast about it. Not many people in Rome knew or cared about war crimes. It was winning that mattered. Of course, it looked different from the barbarian point of view, but the barbarians got very little chance to put their point of view at Rome.

But even in the ancient world, it wasn't quite so simple. Many modern observers of the column of Marcus Aurelius (the 'other', less famous column still standing in the centre of the city) have wondered just how 'subversive' were the scenes of Roman violence depicted. The theme is Marcus Aurelius' campaigns against the Germans. There is much more here than on Trajan's column of (for example) women and children getting abducted or slaughtered. Was this all celebratory? Or was there at least a strand here of displaying (even if not directly questioning) the very nasty side of Roman conquest?

And as for leaks, the problems of communication in the ancient world meant that there were leaks and rumours aplenty. This is one of the things that struck me most when I was researching my book *The Roman Triumph*. I discovered that the senate often said to a general returning home and wanting a triumphal procession that they would wait and interview some of the (Roman) eye-witnesses before deciding on whether the victory deserved such an honour. The most extraordinary rumour I came across concerned a victory scored by Cassius Longinus (who went on to be one of the assassins of Julius Caesar). He claimed to have repelled an invasion of Parthians into Syria. Had he? One rumour circulating in Rome was that they weren't Parthians at all but Arabs dressed up as Parthians. (A bit like us saying that they weren't the Taliban but a load of Kurds dressed up as Taliban.)

And civilian losses could be controversial too.

Of course, what counted as 'civilians' could have been rather different in antiquity. In a sense, given the nature of ancient military service, all adult males counted as soldiers – so civilians were the women and children. Which of these, and exactly how many, should be a casualty of war was famously debated by the Athenians in the middle of the Peloponnesian War. After they had put down a revolt in the city of Mytilene on the island of Lesbos, they at first decided to kill all the

male citizens and enslave all the women and children. But the
next day they debated the question again and took a different
view (admittedly on grounds of expediency rather than
compassion) and decided to execute only the ringleaders of the
revolt.

All the same, the ancient military machine didn't have to
face leaks on the scale we have just seen about Afghanistan.
And a depressing set of documents it seems to be. Never mind
the big things that will come out of this new material; most
of us who have ever raised issues about civilian casualties and
read all those blanket denials will feel pretty angry to discover
that at least some of those denials appear to have been lies. And
in this country, whenever you question the behaviour of the
NATO troops in Afghanistan, you get the 'Wootton Bassett'
card thrown at you ... the 'How could you insult our boys?'

Well, it turns out that some of our boys' bullets (and other
NATO nations' boys' bullets) have killed more civilians than
was ever let on.

But it is more complicated than that, and certainly not a
question of deploring the behaviour of individual soldiers.
The real culprits are those political leaders who convinced us
that you could fight an Afghan guerrilla war without hurting
the innocent as well as the 'guilty'; those who strongly implied
(even if they didn't quite say) that modern warfare could be
surgical and indeed, successfully conducted, could win the
hearts and minds of the decent Afghan people.

Dream on. The Romans were at least more realistic about
war always being very nasty indeed.

Comments

The style guide of the *Guardian* newspaper has this entry:
'innocent civilians: the adjective is superfluous'

MICHAEL BULLEY

Weren't Marcus Aurelius' campaigns against the Germans
defensive rather than offensive?

   I thought that huge waves of German and Samatian tribes
were making serious incursions into Roman provinces, looting,
burning and killing, and the Romans were somewhat desperately
straining every resource to repel them.

MARKS

Given that the Taleban (which is Arabic for 'students', by the way)
are by definition not members of the armed forces of a state, the
word 'non-combatant' would be better. This is not the *Guardian*
anyway!

GEOFFREY WALKER

Taliban is a Persian plural formation of 'talib', the Arabic plural
being 'tullab' or 'talaba'. Arabic 'taliban' would be the dual form:
'two students'. If only.

ANTHONY ALCOCK

The politics of Britain's brainiest cemetery

11 September 2010

I woke up this morning to a great item on the *Today* programme by my colleague Mark Goldie, about the cemetery 100 yards or so up the road from our house, 'Ascension Burial Ground'.

I first went there about 25 years ago, looking for the grave of James Frazer, on whom I was then working (with his fantastic, obsessive anal archive, compiled largely, I suspect, by Lady Frazer and now in the care of Trinity College – on which more in a minute). And have wandered up, every now and then, ever since, doing what my mother used to call 'churchyard creeping' and finding the memorials of the long-lost dons. It's a great place for a Sunday stroll ... and if I had to spend eternity somewhere, it would be my place of choice. (I expect a plot is rather expensive.)

Mark obviously shares my enthusiasm for the Burial Ground, its slightly 'overgrown-ness', its motley crowd of occupants, the striking contrasts and the hints of living character. (As you would expect, that dandy, Sir Richard Jebb's – late nineteenth-century Professor of Greek – monument is a very grand creation.) But he carefully drew a veil over some of the more curious politics, and other weirdnesses, of the place.

Take Wittgenstein's grave (above).

It is, as Mark pointed out, very plain: a simple slab, with just his name and date. Mark put this down to the man himself, his refusal to utter in death as in life anything beyond the verifiable.

Yes, it certainly seems appropriate to the man. But there are other, less noble factors at work here too. Wittgenstein's memorial is actually a pretty close match for that of Sir James and Lady Frazer (who you would expect to have something a bit more showy – Frazer was a real celeb by the 1930s). The secret is that both these slabs must have been commissioned by Trinity College on the cheap. (Rich colleges in Cambridge may look after archives very nicely, but they don't throw their money around on slabs.) Wittgenstein died without heirs, and the Frazers died within a day of each other and without kids – so in both cases it fell to Trinity to handle the funeral and the grave. The fact that it fitted nicely with Wittgenstein's character was a happy coincidence.

But Wittgenstein's grave is even more curious than that. For a start, it attracts a regular series of offerings and tributes. The last time I went, there was a little ladder on it (after his famous metaphor, I suppose) and an assortment of drooping flowers.

There is also a politics of proximity. If one is thinking of eternity, it might seem important to be next to a friend rather than a rival or enemy. And that's exactly what Wittgenstein's pupil Elizabeth Anscombe must have thought. For how else, apart from buying the next-door plot, did she end up in death at Wittgenstein's feet? Even defying the boundaries of religion – for she was a Catholic after all.

Worth a trip, and a ponder on the politics – though, as the husband points out, not quite on the scale of Highgate.

Comments

Mary, I was taught that in English prose an adjective precedes the noun to which it refers. I am amused by the thought that a cemetery can be brainy. Its deceased residents certainly, but the cemetery itself … ??

SUE SKINNER

Sue Skinner – If I were in the condemned cell, my despairing hope would be that you were the planning official responsible for condemning it.

No careless error on Mary's part but hypallage.

TOHU

Another university burial ground worth a side-visit if you are passing near is the Alter Friedhof in Bonn on the Rhine. I used to live just along the same street.

The monumental tomb of Robert and Klara Schumann is most impressive, but you will also find the last resting places of Beethoven's mother and of his violin teacher, the graves of the wife and son of Friedrich Schiller, and the burial place of August Wilhelm Schlegel, translator of Shakespeare, Calderón and the *Ramayana* and one of the founding fathers of linguistics. (Loads of others for those familiar with German literature and history.)

BILLY

Museum parties: balls, dances, conferences and the great and the good

23 September 2010

I have been doing some work in the archives of the Fitzwilliam Museum, and particularly the nineteenth-century history of the place (on which more later). But a very quick trawl produces some eye-opening surprises.

I had always imagined that the idea of holding parties in museums was an invention of (well?) the 1970s. It was, I thought, a consequence of the underfunding of museums, with an added push from a Thatcherite business ethic. Indeed, when the Greeks objected in the 1990s to the British Museum serving sandwiches in front of the Elgin Marbles, I gave them the benefit of the doubt – that the British practice of eating and drinking in front of works of art might actually be new.

I have no idea what happened in the BM in the nineteenth century. But in Cambridge, in the Fitzwilliam, the practice of museum hospitality goes back to before the Museum was fully built.

In July 1842, even before the building was finished, there was a grand royal ball in the shell of the Museum. In addition to a clutch of London royalty, who presumably came 'free', 1,750 tickets were sold in aid of the (then) nearby Addenbrooke's Hospital – dancing went on all night, till 6.00 a.m., and the next morning the loyal hoi polloi were let in to see the detritus for 2s. 6d. It was obviously a pretty glamorous occasion (the walls were hung with bunting and other material in red and white stripes) – but not without its dangers: the *Illustrated London News* reported that the hundreds of candles hung about the place dropped their wax on to the bare shoulders of the ladies, and made a real mess of the men's suits.

But the tradition went on. There was another big-shot gala (this time with the pictures fully installed) in 1864, and a gala lunch provided in the galleries again in 1904, when the King and Queen were in town, not to mention the regular honorary degree lunches too. But there were also rather more cerebral occasions.

By the end of the nineteenth century conferences in Cambridge (and who is one day going to write a history of 'the conference'?) were having conversazioni (plus music and a good deal of refreshment) in the Museum. In 1899, for example, the National Union of Teachers showed up for a reception, with some nice autograph copies of music specially laid out for them to enjoy, in between the Egyptian sarcophagi and the Greek marbles in the basement. A few years earlier, in 1896, there had been a conversazione at a conference on secondary education – with an on-the spot-demonstration of Roentgen rays!

Actually the tradition continues. We are arranging a big Classics conference for next year – and guess where we are having the reception?

The Fitzwilliam.

Comments

Richard Owen organised a dinner in December 1853 inside the reconstructed iguanodon that he had commissioned for the 1851 Great Exposition in Hyde Park.

It's not quite a museum reception, since the Crystal Palace was closed then, but it's close.

BRIAN W. OGILVIE

World-class universities vs. the Human Resources Compliance Unit

14 October 2010

Britain has a good number of world-class universities, and many more than you would expect for its population and GDP. One of the things that *keeps* those universities world-class is the exchange of lectures, seminars, examiners etc. across the globe.

So, reflect on this: just recently a directive has come down to us from the 'management' (as I have regretfully come to call the administration ... only ten years ago they felt like my 'colleagues'), explaining that in future we will only be allowed to appoint external examiners for PhDs from those who have a right to work in the UK (i.e., no Americans, Australians whatever). Apparently, so our 'Human Resources Compliance Unit' (I am not joking) assures us, reading a PhD thesis, writing a report and giving the candidate a viva of (say) two hours counts as 'employment'. So if you are appointed to do this, you need to prove your eligibility to work in this country, by showing your passport.

If this is correct (and I mean *if*), then this is just one little blow to the idea of the UK as a home of world-class scholarship.

In my Faculty, we normally use UK scholars to examine PhDs (we don't squander travelling expenses), but sometimes students have been researching subjects that really do require a non-EEA examiner. Tony Grafton of Princeton, for example, may be one of the very few people in the world properly qualified to examine a specialised PhD – but he would no longer be appointable, at least on this interpretation of the law. And indeed it is lucky that the recently appointed 'Australian' examiner, who has just taken on one of our theses, turned out to have a UK passport.

So what are our options? Well, HR seems to offer none. (So much for being a world-class university at the cutting edge of international research … or should we now say 'European' research.) One idea in my neck of the woods is that we do it all by video link, so that the examiner doesn't have to come into the country. (So much for those face-to-face exchanges of views that make academic life worth living and top-notch.) Another is that we fly the candidate and the external examiner to the US or Australia or wherever. Or maybe we just use the Channel Islands.

This is a just tiny example of new immigration madness. But the idea that the best students in Cambridge should not be examined by the best and most appropriate scholars in the world *must* make mockery of our claim to be one of the top universities on the planet (for that is what the international community of scholars is all about). And indeed why should reading a PhD thesis count as 'employment' anyway? Could our HR department have actually got this wrong?

The next thing they will be telling us is that when we invite people to give our prestige-endowed lectures, we will only be able to invite those with a right to work here.

This can't be what the immigration legislation intended. But, for what it is worth, any university which asks me to produce my passport before I accept the 100 quid for a minimum of 25 hours work examining a PhD thesis can BOG OFF.

Comments

Anyone remember the 'Protect & Survive' leaflet?

Our last remaining export is ideas. Thinking. 'Intellectual property.' Now we've given up. We're closing it all down. Pin the blankets over the windows, make a nice cup of tea, under the stairs with a paper bag over our heads and wait quietly to die.

MICHAEL BYWATER

It may be what the legislation intended, but more likely it merely exemplifies, what I have long suspected to be the fact, that no one in the civil service understands elementary Aristotelian logic, otherwise they would have seen the implications while the relevant bill was still in the drafting stage.

When I was at school (too long ago to contemplate) we had classes in 'Use of English' which involved (among other things) applying elementary logic to English texts – but I guess that has all gone by the board nowadays. One wonders: is there anyone in Whitehall capable of recognising, let alone producing, a syllogism?

DAVID KIRWAŃ

People in Whitehall don't know what a syllogism is? That's terrible. I must send them one at once. Let's see. How about this?

A work permit allows you to work in Britain.

Mary Beard isn't a work permit.

Therefore Mary Beard doesn't allow you to work in Britain.

MICHAEL BULLEY

May I say how hateful these regulations are? Examining students in Cambridge and London has brought me extraordinary benefits – friendships and exchanges with brilliant young scholars whom I wouldn't otherwise have known, for a start. And I've done my best to help the examinees with detailed reports on what they wrote and letters of recommendation and the like afterwards. Many of my colleagues have done this as well – in fact, more often in recent years than in the past – and they too have profited and helped others. It's very sad to see this small but vital part of academic cosmopolitanism destroyed.

TONY GRAFTON

Doesn't it seem like we – this once rebellious generation – are becoming a bit cowed by this onslaught of administration? Having no respect for these rules and their enforcers, I think a little legerdemain may be in order.

Do you all trot down to the council to get the necessary permissions for all the repairs in your homes? Never a little black market traffic in the odd plumbing, electrical or decorating job?

It seems to me that you need to start padding your expenses and lay in a store of cash. When a check isn't possible, an envelope with a few hundred pound notes would do quite nicely.

LEX STEVENS

The good news is that shortly after this post was published, HR decided that PhD examiners did not need to apply for visas!

Bedding down in the Library

30 October 2010

Earlier this week I took part in a debate at the British Library – 'Is the Physical Library a Redundant Resource for Twenty-First-Century Academics' – organised by *Times Higher Education*. To put it another way, should we all stay at home/in our studies and call up all the resources we need on our laptops and let the country save all the money that bricks and mortar and bulky things like books eat up.

Now no one could accuse The Don of being a Luddite (I have my laptop open in the breakfast table and can't imagine what life was like before JSTOR), but I don't intend to give up the physical library without a jolly good fight.

My paean of praise for the physical library included some of the familiar lines … You don't just go to the library for information, you go there to learn how to think differently, and that is about ordering, classification, serendipity (what book you find on the shelf next to the one you thought you were looking for). And you go also for the people, the other readers and the librarians. And you go for the sheer pleasure of having space and quiet to *think*, not to mention the pleasures of transgression. And on this topic I had a little nostalgic reflection on all the things we used to do in libraries … eat, drink, smoke substances legal and illegal, have sex. I was tempted to ask for a show of hands from those who had ever made love in a library bookstack, a bibliophile's Mile High club, but thought embarrassment might produce a misleadingly low score.

In case any younger readers are puzzled, smoking used
to be allowed in libraries a few years ago. Again a bit like on
planes, the back two tables of the Cambridge Classics Library
used to be the smoking tables, and the husband recalls how the
Warburg Library went on allowing smoking well after other
London libraries. Banning it would have caused a riot among
its elderly Eastern European readers but did – he points out
– make the place a bit whiffy for everyone else. (Health and
Safety gurus might like to reflect that none of these libraries
burned down!)

In some ways the most interesting area of disagreement
between myself and the other panellists was in terms of
speed and 'academic output'. There is little doubt that a lot
of information can be more quickly retrieved electronically.
Most of the other speakers treated this as an unproblematic
good, and one went so far as to relate our embracing of new
technology to the fact that UK academics produce more
outputs per head than those of other nations.

At this point I felt very much in the opposite corner. The
fact is that really good thinking is often a very *slow* process ...
and it is the kind of process that goes on when you are waiting
the 30 minutes that it takes for the book to arrive on your
table, or on the 15-minute (for me) bike ride to the library.
Indeed, speed of information retrieval can actually work
against good thinking. (Should we, I wondered, start a *slow
thinking* movement like slow cooking ... ?)

And as for congratulating ourselves on producing more
than other nations ... it's quality we want, not quantity. We
probably should slow down a bit.

Anyway, by a nice coincidence I am now in New York for
some meetings. And I am staying in The Library Hotel ... a
niche market hotel near New York Public Library – and on

a library theme. All the rooms are numbered according to the Dewey decimal system and are kitted out with books to match. (I'm in Management 600.003, which isn't too much of a temptation, but the husband had philosophy a couple of weeks ago.)

A Library where eating, drinking, sleeping – but not smoking, of course – are all encouraged.

Comments

I recall people smoking in even the most hallowed of libraries – including eye-wateringly strong shag tobacco – I missed out on that other indulgence between the stacks. Altho' there were corners to fall asleep in, undetected. Libraries aren't as quiet as they used to be. I haven't heard a librarian hiss 'Shhh!' in aeons.

JANE-ANNE SHAW

Ah yes, smoking. When the Cambridge University Library tea room was in the South Courtyard, there was a smoking room near where one went in, that is, away from the counter. I think that the glass partition was eventually taken down, the ceiling cleaned and smoking indoors prohibited.

According to the rules, smoking in the courtyards is still allowed. As for sex, you must do it quietly (rule 14), not use any equipment that might disturb or distract other readers (rule 17), not prejudice anyone's safety, well-being or security or the preservation of the collections (rule 24) and keep your socks on (rule 23).

RICHARD BARON

I don't believe that smoking was allowed in any library 'a few years ago'. Sprinkler systems have been around for quite a bit, and while the smoke itself does no damage to the books, water certainly can. I lit up once in the Griffith Institute (Oxford) library back in the early '70s and a gentle spray began to descend, but the sprinkler was turned off in time. No damage was done. If the library allows people to eat, thorough cleaning is necessary to avoid vermin. Many people nod off at their desks. I used to do it regularly. EO James used to bring an alarm clock into the Griffith to wake him up.

ANTHONY ALCOCK

For those of us who are not subsidised by the taxpayer, as opposed to just being, um, the taxpayer, it's quite easy to imagine life without JSTOR, as we are still living it.

MARK

Smoking in the Widener or Houghton (or any other) libraries at Harvard in the nicotine-infused era of the 1950s was simply not done. I doubt that has changed. I can only note that I once smelled the smoke of the weed that appeared to come from the nook (many on each floor of the stacks) of a distinguished scholar.

JAMES WADE

Students occupy the Senate House

1 December 2010

As I write, the student occupation of the Senate House in Cambridge is entering its sixth day. To be precise, they are occupying the University Combination Room – which is a wise decision, as it is a large room, has a lot of comfy chairs, a controversial lift and won't be much missed by most working senior members of the university, who haven't got a minute to take a coffee break/lunch there anyway.

They are protesting against the now usual combination of 'fees and cuts'. Am I on their side?

Well, in one way, of course I am. It would be worrying if the students (and sixth-formers with some eye on the future) didn't see what government proposals were likely to do to higher education, to the realistic chances of the less well-off going to university (the coalition can go on till it's blue in the face about how there is nothing to pay up front, but the likelihood is that £30–40k of debt will put off many of the kids we want to attract), and to the strength of Arts and Humanities in particular (which can't possibly operate successfully on a supply and demand model). So, yes, they are right to make a fuss.

And anyone who looks at what the students have been doing in the Combination Room can hardly help but be touched: vegan meals, poetry readings, improving lectures, art-house movies and a good deal of essay-writing. In those terms, and let's hope this continues, it's a model of student protest. If I was 30 years younger (and didn't have getting on for 20 hours teaching to be done in the rest of this week), I'd be there.

My only worry is what it is actually going to achieve, and who is to be convinced about what. And more generally, what the academic community in general should be doing to get their point across most effectively about this damage that is being done.

The students are trying to convince the university authorities. But, by and large, the authorities are broadly on the same side as the students (even if they have rather different ways of getting there). And the full range of student demands are probably not something any authorities could agree to anyway, not to the letter ('That the university declare it will never privatise' ... never say never). Interestingly the supporting letter from academics (which I have just signed) stops far short of backing the full student manifesto: the letters asks the university to 'take note' of the student demands, and the Vice-Chancellor to express opposition to the current government's destructive agenda.

But on the other hand, what are the students supposed to do? If they have a peaceful little march through the city centre and go back to their rooms, then the government pats itself on the back for smiling benevolently on the citizens' right to peaceful protest, and takes not a blind bit of notice.

So what is the right answer? I'm not sure. There have been some good things said in television debates about what the reforms will mean for arts and humanities (close to death, being the answer) ... but our spokespeople do tend to look like rather languid Oxbridge types.

And some of us did send a letter to the *Telegraph*, the Tory party paper of choice (asking for a public inquiry 'on the future of higher education' and muttering about 'considerable unease'). Let's hope someone reads it.

Comments

Not one of the students' spokespeople we have heard has said a single word about Britain's economic situation. It is rather like 1947–50 all over again with the Chiefs of Staff calling for thousands of troops, garrisons, equipment etc. to be allocated around the 'empire' to maintain our world-class position (*sic*!) without any reference to the uncomfortable fact that the country was technically bankrupt.

PETER WOOD

I am glad to hear that essays are being written in the University Combination Room. The eye-witness report I received from the Lower Radcliffe Camera in Oxford was of tap-dancing on the book issue desk and other oafish behaviour making it impossible for people to get on with their work.

OLIVER NICHOLSON

'My only worry is what it is actually going to achieve.' This line of argument is morally bankrupt. Sometimes a gesture is worth making even if it achieves nothing. Remember the parable of the woman who shields her child from a hail of bullets with her arm – George Orwell discusses it in *Nineteen Eighty-Four*. The gesture achieves nothing, but it is still the right thing to do.

DOCTORENO

Student occupation: the dilemmas

5 December 2010

OK – as the *TLS* editor and others have pointed out following my last post, having an awful lot of teaching to do is not much of an excuse for failing to get my hands dirty down at the occupation at the Old Schools. ('Where were you when the revolution needed you, Beard … ?' 'Teaching, Sir … ')

But that is just one of the paradoxes of this kind of political action.

I mean, if the students are protesting (in part) in order to save the study of Arts and Humanities from the forces of darkness, then there would have been something self-destructive in giving up the teaching of said subjects, just to join in at the Senate House.

And especially this week, when I was seeing all the third-years for whom I Direct Studies, one by one, as well as checking in with those whose undergraduate theses I am supervising, squeezing in the last essay supervision of the term with everyone else and making sure that the MPhils get their first assessed essays in in time … etc. etc. (If you ever hear any Mum or Dad complain that their kid is not getting the hands-on treatment at Uni that they expected – don't believe it; at least not for Classics in Cambridge.)

Anyway, this all coincided with the long-listing meeting for our college junior research fellowship competition – which meant reading carefully through 218 applications to pick out fewer than 20 to go to the next stage (in the end we have only one position to give). You can do the calculations for yourself.

Just imagine I took the bare minimum of 10 minutes per application (and that would have been a cracking pace) – it would have taken 36 hours solid … indeed it did, and more.

But there are other strange anomalies. And the biggest of those is the very nature of the law-breaking and transgression that the occupation implies.

Let me repeat that, politically, I am absolutely on the side of the students; they are standing up for a load of principles in which I believe. And I hope that the University lets them off very lightly indeed, and gets down to talk to them about the issues and dilemmas we are facing. For the students are our greatest allies.

But, all the same, there is something illogical in thinking (as some of my colleagues seem to do) that any threat of punishment or legal action is merely an example of the oppressive and vindictive power of establishment authority being wreaked on the innocent.

After all the students are occupying a place in contravention of custom, rule and law. That's the whole point. You can't 'occupy' somewhere (like a JCR, or Students' Union) where you are allowed to be anyway. It *has* to be transgressive; and so it has to attract the attention (yes, and even the threats) of the authorities and the police, who in their turn have to make it clear that transgression is taking place. Otherwise it's more like a sleepover than a protest.

There is, in other words, a symbiosis here between action and reaction, protest and punishment, that goes unnoticed in many of the cries of anguish we are now hearing about the authorities' tough line.

It reminds me of when my son, a sixth-former, bunked off school to march against the Iraq war. I was dead proud of him.

Then the school rang to say that he had been absent without leave.

Yes, I said, and I hope that you will be punishing him. No, came the reply, he is very sincere.

Sincere or not, I thought, there was a lesson to be learned here. If you want to protest, that's fine, but you have to feel the pinch – otherwise it's too risk-free, and you are being smothered in well-meaning paternalism. ('Off you go and march now/occupy the Old Schools … just so long as you are "sincere".)

In my son's case, I would have had him do 500 lines: 'Mr Blair is wrong to go to war on Iraq' 500 times over would, I think, have been an appropriate punishment in the circumstances.

For our students, I would pat them on the back, give them a very big cheer and a party – then I would have them give 20 hours to a telephone campaign raising money for Arts and Humanities, or writing begging letters to old boys and girls explaining why they had occupied the Old Schools, why it was important to them and why a bit of cash would help.

It's called making the 'punishment' fit the 'crime'.

Comments

There was the odd teach-in at German universities in the events leading up to the hallowed '1968'. Those in attendance at the first one c. 1966 in West Berlin (as it was then) had to listen to Rudi Dutschke on the subject of anti-authoritarianism. A woman I got to know later, who had attended some of these performances, told me that at the revolutionary meetings the boys demanded that the girls get the coffee and sandwiches ready and do the washing up later on.

ANTHONY ALCOCK

Can black kids get into Cambridge?

7 December 2010

I confess, I have escaped to Rome (to the American Academy). The idea was to do some of the research which is my job. The truth is that I have spent most of the last 24 hours answering emails and writing references.

Since I left Cambridge, the students have ended their occupation of the administration building. (Well done, one and all, for keeping our eyes on what will happen to Arts and Humanities if the government proposals have their way.) And then the *Guardian* had an exposé of how few black students get into Oxbridge.

Can I stick up for us, again? There can be no sensible person who thinks that it is OK that 21 Oxbridge colleges took no black student last year. But before we go down the 'Oxbridge snobs aren't interested in most of the ordinary kids of this country' route, can we stop to think? Oxbridge bashing is often a convenient alibi for not reflecting on what the bigger problem is … it's easier to dump on racist Oxbridge dons than to fix some of the big things that might be the matter with state education.

Let me put a few points:

1) The figures quoted by the *Guardian* were about black students, not about ethnic 'minorities' over all … Asian, Middle Eastern etc. It is true that the number of black Afro-Caribbean students at Cambridge is woefully low, but that is not the case with other ethnic 'minorities'.

Obviously it varies from subject to subject, but it is simply not true that Cambridge is a middle-class white place. My college (Newnham) came out badly in the number of black students it took, measured by proportion of applicants to places ... but I defy anyone to come and say that it 'feels' white.

2) The figures are always more complicated than they seem. There is no single variable when it comes to 'getting in' (however much it suits journalists to pretend that there is) – you need to factor race against class and school/educational background etc. before you get a start at understanding what is going on. On this scoring, Kwasi Kwarteng (black Etonian, ex-Trinity) counts for ethnic diversity (true, but not exactly what most of us mean by 'access').

3) There are other ways in which you need to break the figures down. As the *Guardian* article was honest enough to point out, more than 29,000 white students got three As or better at A level; fewer than 500 black students did (though nearly 50% of those applied to Oxbridge, whereas fewer than 30% of the white students did). There is also a subject bias – in that black students disproportionately applied for the most competitive subjects. (Though that is tricky again: the fact that there are fewer applicants per place for Classics than for most other subjects does not mean that it is a back-door route to Oxbridge for the privileged ... kids who have chosen Latin and Greek have always 'pre-selected' themselves, no matter what their backgrounds.)

4) I have to say that I haven't seen racism in Cambridge admissions – far from it. I know that the answer to that is that institutional racism is invisible, so of course I wouldn't have noticed it. But the fact is that we DO get training in

interviewing, so that we don't just wreak our prejudices.
And the university has a great campaign (GEEMA – that is,
'Group to Encourage Ethnic Minority Applications'). A lot
of people put a lot of time into this. Simplistic conclusions
of the 'Oxbridge is racist' variety only make their job more
difficult.

And I don't think that it is true.

Comments

Can black kids get into Cambridge? Not as easily as white kids.
MIKE

When I was at Girton, there were women of all skin colours there.
As a farm girl from Yorkshire, I was probably more exotic than
they.
OURSALLY

A pig for a present

25 December 2010

It is 8.oo in the morning on Christmas day, and I haven't yet opened my presents, which still wait around the tree until the turkey is safely in oven. (There was a minor hiccough last night when a fault in the electronic clock appeared to make it impossible to turn the oven ON – could you grill a turkey in pieces, we started to wonder? – but a bit of fiddling with the buttons sorted the problem.)

But one particular present has already made an impact.

Last Friday the husband texted me in Rome to say that there was a bit of a problem with an unexpected gift which had arrived at college. It was a suckling pig, which would not fit in the freezer … vegetarians, please don't read on.

As it happened, if I had known the cold weather would last, it could just have sat in the garden for a week or so, until we cooked it. (That was, of course, another challenge, given the

size of our oven, even when working.) But being on the safe
side, I decided to find it a temporary home in a big freezer …
So I made a mercy call to our butchers (the estimable Waller
and Son, of Victoria Avenue in Cambridge), and they took it in
for the weekend.

But where next? College was the obvious answer, so as
soon as I was back from Italy, I drove to the butcher and
took it round to Newnham. The trouble about that was that
the catering manager was a generous host to the pig, but the
kitchens would be entirely closed between 23 December and
5 January, and there would be no space for the beast after the
10th. So if I was planning to cook it (how?) over the festive
season, it would be inaccessible.

Anyway, one of the advantages of getting older in a town
like this is that you get to have friends who are institutionally
equipped with big fridges and big ovens. So, explaining the
problem to my friends Andrew and Jo (Mr and Mrs Sidney
Sussex College), it quickly became clear that the Master's
Lodge offered a solution to all problems … a big freezer and a
big oven, and we all turned out to be free on New Year's Day,
on which occasion the animal could be cooked and consumed.

So I went and collected it from Newnham and drove the
beast to Sidney, where Jo and I received a lesson from the Head
Chef on how long to defrost him (her?) for before cooking,
and what gas mark was required etc. etc. And so we are all set.

And indeed not only has the pig given me a birthday party,
but it has made a wide impact around the town. No sooner do
I go into college than they ask about its fate, and when I went
into the butcher's to pick up the turkey, one of the Waller's men
said, 'Andrew's looking forward to eating the pig' … how did
he know? Well, he turned out to be the acting head porter of

Sidney … and had been filled in on the fate of the beast from many sides!

So thanks to the semi-anonymous donor (Patrick x x x x x x what a star you are!), and to all who have helped out (especially Jo and Andrew).

On other fronts, Christmas set to go … we even have a little tree in the new bathroom!

What's wrong with government by petition?

28 December 2010

There was huffing and puffing round the breakfast table this morning as we listened to the government's new gimmick – that successful on-line petitions should get a parliamentary debate, and even made into a bill. The Labour MP (Paul Flynn) had some sensible things to say about the idea … but as the husband pointed out, it's a pity the Labour Party hadn't been more sensible when they started this whole e-petition idea. It was, after all, their gimmick in the first place.

So what is the matter with the idea?

Well, for a start, it is a veneer of popular power, a substitute touted as the real thing. Mass e-petitioning looks as if it is putting power back into the people's court. But actually it is more likely to give an outlet to the computer-literate, with time on their hands and an axe to grind (which is a decidedly skewed sub-category of 'the people'). Remember how the *Today* programme had to stop its annual 'person of the year' competition because all kinds of maverick campaigns launched all kinds of very odd people into the top of the list.

Second, it is taking us in the wrong direction in terms of legislative activity. What we need is less legislation, fewer white papers – not more. That is to say, we need a bit more sense that the solution to every problem is not a new law. This e-petition idea risks turning us all into amateur lawmakers.

And finally, it turns the complexity of politics into a competition between single-issue interest groups (and that in the long term has the effect of taking power away from 'the people', not giving it back). Of course we would all like to save the sparrows and the bees, stop rape and have a better public transport system ... and no doubt you could get hundreds of thousands of people to sign up for those causes. But the real politics is not about signing up to some obvious good causes, it's about balancing and prioritising a competing selection of good causes. That's what, for us, the parliamentary process is all about. And anyone who wants to see the fatuity of the petition mode could well study the fruitless Californian system of 'propositions', which serve to paralyse more than enhance government.

So far, I guess, so obvious.

But a quick look at the Downing Street 'petition' site only makes one even gloomier – if for rather different reasons.

For a start, it's not clear that in practice this government gimmick is offering very much. Unless the site was having a hiccough over Christmas, there appear to be no current, open petitions at all (maybe people are fed up with the Labour gimmick already).

And of the closed petitions, I reckoned that since 2007 only eight got over the magic figure of 100,000 that would give them any parliamentary time. Three were about fuel and other motoring issues (and I don't think that these were being neglected, even without a petition ... MPs aren't *that* unrepresentative!), one was about creating a military hospital, another about having a Remembrance Day public holiday and another about letting the Red Arrows fly past at the 2012 Olympics. The other two were asking for the abolition of

inheritance tax (128,622 signatures) and the abolition of plans
to build a 'Mega Mosque' (281,882).

Now some of this amply confirms the arguments I sketched
in the first part of this post. I have no idea what campaign was
driving the more than half a million signatories who wanted
to see the Red Arrows at the Olympics, but as a rather pained
government response makes clear, they hadn't been banned
from appearing anyway:

> This allegation is not true. The Government has not
> banned the Red Arrows from the London 2012 Olympic
> Games. The organising committee of London 2012 will
> decide what to include in the Opening Ceremony and
> other celebrations – but with almost five years to go,
> decisions are yet to be made on what these will look like.

And, as for the inheritance tax lobby, this is exactly the
kind of single-issue campaigning that gets in the way of
joined-up financial thinking. (So where do they want to find
the money that is 'lost' to the public purse?)

But a closer look at the website gives a different slant. The
whole thing is so monitored that it is only the 'voice of the
people' in a terribly sanitised way. The most depressing part is
the list of 'rejected petitions' – those that have been deemed
off-limits, not qualifying for a response. There are more than
38,000 of these – more than the total of those allowed through
the system.

And what have they done wrong? In some cases they
have talked about things that people really care about, but
are sub judice or outside the Prime Minister's remit. ('It is
not appropriate to petition the PM regarding legal cases over
which he has no jurisdiction.') Or they have written rather too
frankly. A whole host get the chop because they 'contained

language which is offensive, intemperate, or provocative'.
(Well, offensive is one thing … but are we not allowed to be
provocative in a petition?) Others are banned because they
contained links to websites (so much for new technology),
were funny, or because they 'contained party political material'
… err isn't this part of the political process?

So much for letting the people have their say. I can't stand
this gimmicky idea anyway, but if I did think that it gave us,
the public, some direct influence over the political process, a
good look at the website would make me think I'd been short-
changed.

Comments

According to the BBC website, one of Paul Flynn's comments was:
'The blogosphere is not an area that is open to sensible debate;
it is dominated by the obsessed and the fanatical, and we will
get crazy ideas coming forward'. It is a great comfort to know that
Government and Parliament are not at all like that.

RICHARD BARON

The Classical precedents for popular power in politics are not
encouraging: was it not popular power that exiled Anaxagoras
on a charge of heresy (for saying that the sun was a red-hot rock
somewhat bigger than the Peloponnese) and condemned Socrates
to drink hemlock?

DAVID KIRWAN

Petitions may not be a good idea, but good old Ostracism might
be worth giving a try …

TOM TILLEY

To tweet or not to tweet?

8 January 2011

I have just signed up to a Twitter account. Many people (including some commenters) had urged me in this direction. But, in the end, the reason I took the plunge was very simple. Fiona Maddocks had given me a bit of much-needed support on Twitter in the face of AA Gill's review of my *Pompeii* programme and his 'How could someone from Newnham understand a willy?' line. (Let him come to Newnham, I say … There's an invitation, Mr Gill!) I couldn't find her email address to say thanks, so I signed up to Twitter to do it that way.

Soon enough I found had some good friends 'following' me. So what now?

I haven't quite managed to tweet ever since. That's partly because I haven't worked out how to do it from my phone.

But it's partly because I haven't worked out what to say. The world might be interested in whether S Fry is at that minute intending to drop by Starbucks, but sure as anything they are not remotely interested in M Beard's coffee-drinking habits.

I have speculated on a more academic approach … 'just read a great article on the Quindecimviri Sacris Faciundis in *Zeitschrift für Papyrologie und Epigraphik*, but wasn't sure how that would go down. I am tempted by the 'message from the front line of the lecture' – which Charlotte Higgins has done very nicely … 'here I am sitting in Nottingham and Prof X has just said that the Romans didn't cut their toenails'. But I haven't been to any lectures lately.

So what? I am shortly to decamp from Cairo to visit some

Roman sites in Egypt (on the hunt for images of Roman emperors). If you would like to give me some suggestions on what to tweet and how to do it, I will try my best.

Comments

I'll keep following as long as you don't boast or tell us you've just cleaned your teeth and cut your toenails.

SUSANNAH CLAPP

I'm giggling about the notion of the Romans and their toenails. (I'd certainly tweet that if someone said it!) The key thing is reciprocity – I use it as a way of disseminating information, picking up information and making contact with a bunch of people I don't see a lot (or indeed have never met). It's a great way to pass on, or find, interesting reading material via links. It's like being at a crowded cocktail party set in a library (and as such, distracting). Don't tweet that you're making an omelette for lunch is my only advice, unless you have something so devastatingly cool to say about it that it's unmissable.

CHARLOTTE HIGGINS

Tweeted to her
Twitty ways
Has left me
In a baffled daze
With wits like
That I tweet you too,
A little line
From twit to you.

A DENNIS

The Colossi of Memnon? When are graffiti not graffiti?

12 January 2011

I have wanted to see the Colossi of Memnon for ages. These
are two huge statues of the Pharaoh Amenhotep III which have
stood since the fourteenth century BC outside the remains of
his 'mortuary temple' not far from Luxor in southern Egypt. It
isn't their Egyptological history that interests me particularly.
(In fact, even after a few days in Egypt, I'm just as bad as I
ever was at telling my Nefertaris from my Nefertitis ... or my
Amenhoteps from my Akhenatens; and indeed I have been
known to glaze over when having them explained.)

For me these statues are important because they were
a Roman tourist attraction – and it is fun to be gawping at
monuments that Germanicus or Hadrian gawped at a couple
of thousand years ago. Not exactly for the same reasons, it
must be allowed. One of the colossi was especially renowned
in the early Roman empire because, thanks to some damage
(possibly in an earthquake in the first century BC), the effect
of the stone warming up in the morning made the statue emit
a strange sound like singing. The Romans said that it was
not Amenhotep at all, but an image of the hero Memnon,
son of Dawn ... who miraculously sang to greet his mother
each morning. Or, he sang most mornings; there were some
unlucky visitors who didn't hear the singing.

The Romans loved the sound and also finished it off. The statue was repaired in the second century and never sang again.

Predictably, perhaps, the tourist guides here (who have never heard of Memnon) tell a brave new version of the story … that they were believed to be statues of AGAmemnon, who wept at dawn. In such ways new myths are born.

Anyway, I had long known that the upmarket Roman visitors did not just admire the sound; they scratched their appreciation in the stone of the figure's huge leg. There are some notable verses: for example, by a lady in Hadrian's party (Julia Balbilla) recording her appreciation in several lines of vaguely Sapphic verses.

I have always called these 'graffiti' before. But a visit has shown that that is quite the wrong way of looking at them. For a start, Julia Balbilla could hardly have improvised her careful Sapphic lines when she arrived and heard the statue perform. She almost certainly came with them already up her sleeve (nothing spontaneous here). But just looking at the texts all over the statue's leg suggested that these texts were a very professional operation. They were mostly very neat (not an amateur scrawl at all, and must have taken a good day to complete even for a trained inscriber); and several of them, even allowing for the changing ground level, were so high up that you would require more than a chair to stand on ... something more like a mini-scaffold.

This was not graffiti in the usual sense of the term at all. It was public display writing commissioned by a set of high-ranking Romans, writing themselves on to a famous, semi-mythical Egyptian monument (or, alternatively, an attempt by the locals to commemorate visits by famous foreign dignitaries).

It was funny that we then went on to the temple at Luxor (much of which was also built by Amenhotep III) and saw graffiti of a different sort there ... also of a 'more than meets the eye' kind. The guidebook was very keen on the signature of (Arthur) Rimbaud, the poet and gun-runner, very high up on the wall of one of the furthest chambers ... indicating how much higher the ground level was in the 1880s, at the time of Rimbaud's visit.

What the guidebook didn't say was that there was another Rimbaud signature on another column a few feet away. This aroused a bit of suspicion. Did Rimbaud ever actually go to Luxor? Well, so far as I can tell from web research, he was certainly in Egypt, but only known in the north. Enid Starkie (who appears to have believed that Luxor is near Alexandria) knew of no other evidence than his 'signature' on the temple.

We have ended up with the distinct impression that once Byron had started the tradition of poets carving their signatures into ancient temples, that was not only an encouragement for any old poet to do the same – it was an encouragement for any fan to *forge* the name of their favourite poet on to an appropriately grand antiquity.

Or does someone have some clear, independent evidence that Rimbaud did make it as far as Luxor?

Comments

In his biography of Rimbaud (2000) Graham Robb suggests that AR could have seen Luxor in 1888, but the style of the inscription suggests an earlier date – perhaps a soldier on Napoleon's 1798 expedition. There were at least two other Rimbauds, one of them a looter of shipwrecks. (AR was good at Classics – prizes at the Institut Rossat etc.)

PETER WOOD

A good source of information on graffiti throughout Egypt and the Sudan is Roger De Keersmaecker's Travellers' Graffiti series (ten volumes and counting): www.egypt-sudan-graffiti.be

MARIE E BRYAN

Universities, despots and plagiarism

7 March 2011

I have been in Washington DC, and have only seen the obvious bits of reportage about the resignation of Howard Davies after the row about Gaddafi junior's funding of the LSE.

I have to say that, nasty as Gaddafi senior is now proving himself (again?) to be, I feel rather sorry for Davies. Every government, for the last 30 years at least, has urged universities to chase outside funding; the chances were always going to be that some of it would come from dubious (or worse) sources.

For the fact is that people who make a very, very great deal of money (the kind of money that would significantly fund a university) are often not particularly nice. There are exceptions, but you know what I mean.

Sure, the spectrum is a wide one, and it runs from the criminal to the merely ruthless. At one end there are the Gaddafis, the arms dealers and fraudsters (as well, if you like, as the tobacco companies). At the other are those who had a brilliant idea or a timely patented invention *plus* the drive to market and exploit it. Clever ideas on their own don't make people rich; it's clever ideas combined with a capacity to corner the market that does it.

Send universities (or museums, or whoever) chasing those multi-billionaires – licensed begging, the husband calls it – and sooner or later you will find they have been tapping into a Gaddafi. It's hypocritical, when that happens, to point the finger. (I'm not sure if ethical fund-raising is any more feasible than an ethical foreign policy.)

I feel conflicted on this one. Half of me wants nothing to do with it and thinks that we should fund universities etc. properly from the public purse (however ethically tainted that may or may not be). The other half thinks that getting money from the bad and turning it to good ends might be a positive thing to do. I certainly suspect that many of the founders of Cambridge colleges acquired their cash in decidedly dubious ways, but we have been doing good with their ill-gotten gains for centuries. In a way, that counts as a moral transformation.

The other issue has been the spotlight on Gaddafi junior's PhD: plagiarised or not? I certainly haven't seen enough to know, but I was taken aback by an article by Lord Desai in the *Guardian* on Friday. He was one of the PhD examiners and he wrote: 'No one at this stage [i.e., when he examined it] had said there were problems of authorship or plagiarism with the thesis.'

I had always thought that determining authorship and originality was one of the jobs of the PhD examiner.

Comments

From you of all people, Mary, I would have expected a reference to Vespasian here: 'Pecunia non olet' ('Money doesn't smell').
MARION DIAMOND

The most contemptible thing about the plagiarism aspect is that no one cared a rat's behind about it when it was expedient to be on good terms with Gaddafi. But when it was suddenly all right to denounce him, people raised their hands in sanctimonious horror at the dishonesty of his son.
BOB

BAFTAs and Emmys

12 May 2011

My good news is that the *Pompeii* programme I was involved
with (made by Brave New Media, Lion TV, with the BBC) has
been short-listed for a BAFTA (Specialist Factual category).
Whatever happens at the next stage, that is jolly good news
for all of us involved. And it's a reassuring confirmation that
people can really appreciate programmes about Pompeii that
do not feature CGI versions of exploding volcanoes or B-grade
actresses dressed up in revealing Roman kit pouring out the
Falernian from a reconstructed Roman bar.

No; instead it was me and Andrew Wallace-Hadrill down
a real ancient sewer talking about the real ancient shit and the
historical secrets it could divulge. The ancient world up close
and personal, and without the distracting frills.

Anyway this means that I will probably get to go along to
the ceremony later in the month, where the final winners are
announced; and to act the star-struck academic in the midst of
the celebrity soap stars, the leading actors from *Downton Abbey*,
plus Stephen Fry. ('Specialist factual', I have quickly realised, is a
bit of a minnow of a category compared with 'comedy'.)

The son and daughter are worried that it will be wasted on
me, as I won't recognise enough people to make it worthwhile.
(I haven't even been watching much *Casualty* lately, which
used to be my regular weekly hospital soap.)

But if our experience at the Emmys is anything to go by, it
will be fun anyway. We got invited to their awards ceremony a
couple of years ago by a friend who organises it … and apart

from Mary Tyler Moore and Tina Fey and *The Late Show*, the hundreds of names and the faces and the shows getting awards were an almost complete mystery to us.

It lasted for hours, and I was particularly worried that the husband, whose tolerance of soaps (particularly those set in American suburbs) is rather less than mine, would not enjoy it a bit. Quite the reverse, though. We were both absolutely gripped by the choreography of it and the whole razzmatazz … and that was before the gala dinner.

So I have high hopes for the BAFTAs, win or no-win.

Comments

SPEECH! SPEECH!
Gosh! I'm so
Shocked, My
Heart's almost
Stopped,
My legs are
Like jelly,
My voice has
Near flopped,
But thank you
So kindly,
So warmly …
God Blimey,
With praise
To 'the husband'
The crew, and
Almighty.
A DENNIS

The sentence for 'serious' rape?

19 May 2011

The most depressing thing about the most recent version of the 'rape debate' is the way it has come down to how long the rapist should be banged up for. The worse we think the crime, the longer they should spend in clink. For what?

On the *Today* programme this morning Vera Baird was attacking the proposal that rapists who pleaded guilty should have a 50% sentence reduction. The argument was that if the average sentence for a rapist was 5 years, then a 50 % reduction meant 2.5 years, which with remission for good behaviour would mean 15 months. Just 15 months, she said … for rape?

Well, there are all kind of factors to weigh up here. As Ken Clarke has pointed out, the 'average' sentence includes those sentenced for 'statutory rape', for any sexual encounter with those aged under 16, however consensual. So the 5-year average is already an odd, and far from 'average', figure.

But leaving those figures aside, and assuming the 15-months sentence, is that a fair punishment?

That's where the 'bang 'em up' mentality seems hopelessly misguided. Most websites today have deplored the idea that a rapist should be let out in under 2 years. WOT 15 months for rape?

No one stopped to say… well 15 months in the nick, that means total loss of job, probable mess of any family relationship, disintegration of family itself (i.e., punishment for them), plus the conversion of a wrongdoer into a hardened criminal (that's what prisons do). Well done, judicial system.

Can't we think of something more humane and better and more designed to stop them doing it again? Isn't there something we can do better for the victim as well as the perpetrator?

Now before you say: you wouldn't say that if you had been raped ... let me say I have been raped – an unwilling encounter on an Italian train that I wrote about years ago in the *London Review of Books*. On the Clarke scheme, it was slightly less than the most serious, but not at the bottom of the heap. I have to say that I agree with him that there are gradations in this crime. I didn't think of going to the police but, if I had, I would have thought that my rapist deserved far less a penalty than if he had jumped at me with a knife or a gun. (I never felt in mortal danger.)

And if I had pressed charges, I don't actually think that I would have wanted the guy banged up. I really, really would like him not to have done it again, and I would have liked to have got the chance to tell him what a tosser he was ... but I don't think I would have wanted to have ruined his life, as he didn't – in the end – ruin mine.

I know I may be tougher in all sorts of ways that other victims of rape; but that doesn't mean that my views shouldn't be heard too. The thought that he would have been in a jail for years would not have been my dream or desire. I would much have much preferred that he spent a long series of weekends picking up rubbish in a seedy Italian town, or using his skills (he was an architect) for free, in the city planning of Italy. Or actually just saying sorry. (If that biscuit factory architect is reading this, he still can say sorry ...)

But overall it has been a bad week for those of us who worry about the modern obsession with imprisonment. The *Today* programme also revealed that the maximum penalty for passing off penalty points for speeding on to someone else was life imprisonment (it's perverting the course of justice).

Have we all lost our marbles?

Comments

I must say I found this blog hard to swallow. Do you mean that if a criminal makes his or her victim feel as if they are mortally endangered, they deserve the clink, where as if they make them feel humiliated, exploited (sensations that might not have applied to your experience but are felt by many rape victims) and traumatised to the extent that she/he wakes up in a rage decades later, this does not require a comparable punishment?

JOSEPHINE

Not winning a BAFTA (… phew???)

23 May 2011

Last night was BAFTA night. The *Pompeii* documentary that I had been part of was nominated for an award in the Specialist Factual category … so we all got dressed up in our best to go to the awards ceremony at the Grosvenor House Hotel.

Needless to say, I am not a regular at this kind of event, and found myself full of both admiration and loathing at the whole slickness of organisation. I met up with some members of the team (Richard, Caterina and Daisy, on her first post-baby outing – just remember, ladies, how wonderful and stressful that is!) in the bar of the Dorchester, before we drove up to the red carpet at the awards HQ.

This is where admiration and loathing kick in. You get out of your car and instantly the ushers know whether to say 'to the left' or 'to the right'. On the left are the paps, with their cameras getting the celebs; on the right are the poor bloody public who have really come to see the celebs but actually get M Beard et al. walking along.

Admiration? Well … it *is* fantastic how these guys instantly know whether you are photo-worthy or not. Loathing? Well, obviously don't get me going on celeb culture.

Inside, after a glass of champagne, I was on a BBC table – with mates and new mates (including Tom Hugh-Jones, son of a Cambridge colleague who made *Human Planet*, nominated in the same category as we were). And we waited till our category prize was announced ('and the BAFTA goes to … ').

We didn't win.

Now let's be honest. If we had won, I would have been very pleased and drunk more champagne than is wise (never mind having to give a lecture at nine o'clock this morning); and would particularly have celebrated the success of those members of the team whose professional award this is. (I guess getting a BAFTA is a bit like becoming an FBA in my day job.)

But was I disappointed? In retrospect, I don't think so. Of course, the whole occasion gears you up to want to win. (That's rather like academic job applications ... you might apply for them when you are young just as a practice run, not expecting to get them, but once you have finished the application, you find you are a bit invested in the whole thing.)

But within a few minutes, I felt a bit of relief.

Look, I thought – this was my first TV programme. It was wonderful – really wonderful – to be nominated for a BAFTA. Actually to win ... that would be a bit different. I mean, I am hoping to do a bit more rather austerely popular, characterful, academic television. How would I have ever lived up to a BAFTA for my first shot at the genre? Wouldn't it always have been a bit of a poisoned chalice?

So thank you all ... I think I have got just the affirmation that I wanted (in fact, more than the approbation and minus the hubris). And I will try to do even better next time.

Comments

Ah, but according to the kitchen cabinet here, you will have to control the producers, insist on a complete absence of distraction, silly sounds off, unnecessary music, remorseless focus etc. And you

will have to be prepared to turn on your heel and walk away if your conditions are not met … *Entsagen Du, sollst Du entsagen!*
PETER WOOD

I have not seen Beard's TV programme, nor do I know the criteria for these awards – many technical/artistic factors are involved, but from what I have gathered from the programme's content I feel some purely academic queries might be raised that diminished its chances. Beard in her usual contrarian way implies the Romans were dirty people and the whole public baths thing was in reality much dirtier than we imagine – people floating around in a kind of oily scum (reminiscent of those jolly British pre-war prep-school days where one was quite liable to find a turd floating by in the communal bath). To support this idea she mentions the lack of drainage – how could the water be kept clean etc. She also mentions how the streets would have been full of refuse and excreta. She also – I believe – looks at modern Naples and observes the refuse disposal problems that continually beset that city. I cannot help thinking that all this shows surely a certain naïveté in approach. Surely a society where three out of five persons were slaves would be able to find some creatures who could be used to sweep these streets clean.
LORD TRUTH/RONALD ROGERS

Young minds ... and the dirty bits (in Aristophanes)

4 June 2011

I am pretty much in agreement with the Mumsnet line that there is something truly ghastly about young kids and aggressively sexualised clothing ... what on earth goes on inside the mind of someone who designs a padded bikini for a six-year-old or a pink T-shirt (size 18 months) with 'Come up and see me some time' blazoned across the front I really can't imagine.

But the David Cameron view, as reported on the radio and in the *Guardian* this morning, prequelling Reg Bailey's recommendations, that it should be banned (along with a whole raft of other things that are 'inappropriate' for kids) is quite another matter. For one thing, how on earth is it going to work? It's all very well being strict on enforcing the nine-o'-clock watershed, but when any self-respecting five-year-old can use iPlayer on his/her computer, what exactly is the point. (And the rules for post-watershed are pretty odd anyway. Our *Pompeii* documentary was a post-watershed programme – and what young minds would that have corrupted?)

And just think of all those lawsuits and legal fees that will follow the disputes about whether this or that logo is too 'sexualised' ... (The point about languages, as Frankie Howerd and Kenneth Williams showed us, is that it is possible to sexualise almost any phrase if you try hard enough.)

But anyway, isn't the effect of a ban (or a brown paper bag around a lad's magazine) to make it more intriguing to the curious child, not less?

That's how it worked when I was 13 or so for the dirty bits in Aristophanes. OK, it took me about a year or so of reading this particular Greek comic poet at school to realise that the reason the line numbers apparently went from 1205 to 1210 in only 3 lines of verse was not to do with problematic and corrupt textual transmission – but because some Victorian nanny-state editor had taken out a possibly corrupting couple of lines that were something to do with sex (or occasionally bottoms).

Their expurgation served to make them much more alluring. So, as soon as we got a chance, and we were up at the boys' school, where they had a much bigger Classical library (thanks to the famous Dr Kennedy – of *The Latin Primer* – among others), we rushed to the unexpurgated version in some complete, not-for-kids, text and pored over it with the boys in a kind of academic version of 'doctors and nurses'. It was, of course, extremely good for our Greek ... but that hadn't been the object of the expurgatory exercise.

Of course, you will object, sexualised clothing and sexualised images near schools are not the same thing as the naughty bits in an ancient Greek dramatist. In some ways they are not – and in some ways they are. Both of them, in their different ways, are a nice illustration of the 'BAN IT' culture that we have come to accept. If you don't like something, if you think – even more –that its presence could harm young minds and bodies, then BAN IT – as if that was effective, and the only strategy of change that there was. Surely, if we disapprove of such things, we are clever enough to devise other ways to discourage them (as at last one sensible report on drug use and abuse suggested this week).

Not every culture behaves in quite this way. When our children were young we often used to spend a week in the summer in a Greek village where there was a nice open-air cinema, usually showing English/US films with Greek subtitles. There was no apparent interest in any form of 'classification', but many of them had '18' certificates over here. The under-10s in the village tended to sit on the front row, enjoying their Coke and ice-creams, while some often up front images of coupling and breasts and bums passed on the screen in front of them (accompanied by a dialogue they couldn't understand and subtitles many of them could not read). Maybe untold damage was being done to them. Who knows? But that was not the impression we got. In fact, most of the younger ones were throughout much more interested in the ice-cream than the screen (on the principle that you have to begin to understand what is going on before you can be interested in it).

Greece isn't exactly a role model in modern Europe at the moment. But this may be something it has got right.

Comments

Interesting. And do you feel the same about 'racism'/'sexism'?
ROGER PEARSE

Lucky it was not a Turkish cinema. I recall a horrific film (being enjoyed by whole families in the open air of a hot Diyarbakir evening) where the baddies put the hero's baby girl on his shoulders placed a noose round her neck, then wrapped the rope round the beam and proceeded to punch the father in the stomach. I could watch no more (to the evident amusement of my kind hosts), but could not fail to catch the bit at the end where the hero uttered the Fatiha and was executed (to tumultuous applause) just BEFORE his grown-up daughter arrived with the reprieve.

OLIVER NICHOLSON

'Many jokes in Aristophanes depend on a fairly detailed knowledge of the physiology and psychology of sex. I have explained these jokes much more plainly than has been the custom hitherto. One reason for this is that, whatever may have been the case in the last century, it is obvious nowadays that most of those who are old enough to study Aristophanes already have a sound factual knowledge of the main line and branch lines of sexual behaviour. A more important reason is my own inability to understand (except in the sense in which one understands a purely historical or anthropological problem) how it could ever have been believed that it was morally objectionable to foster adolescents' appreciation of the more light-hearted aspects of sex but at the same time unobjectionable to acquaint them with the grossest political and forensic dishonesties of the orators.' KJ Dover, *Aristophanes: Clouds* (Oxford: Clarendon Press, 1968), pp. viii–ix.

TERRENCE LOCKYER

Byron noted the 'Aristophanes' effect long ago:

Juan was taught from out the best edition,
Expurgated by learned men, who place,
Judiciously, from out the schoolboy's vision,

The grosser parts; but, fearful to deface
Too much their modest bard by this omission,
And pitying sore his mutilated case,
They only add them all in an appendix,
Which saves, in fact, the trouble of an index.
Byron, *Don Juan*, I.44

HOLT PARKER

Dream School goes to the Education Select Committee

22 June 2011

Yesterday I went to the House of Commons to give evidence at the Education Select Committee, who had decided to discuss what came out of Jamie Oliver's TV *Dream School* experience, where I had taught Latin, and what lessons might be learned. I was a bit sceptical about this. I mean, it was only a reality TV show and – while it might have prompted some interesting debate about things educational – it was not a guide to what is, or is not going on, in the nation's schools. Certainly the idea that you can get any clear idea of issues of discipline from what happens when a TV camera is pointed at 20 late teenagers and a group of (fairly media-hungry) pretend 'teachers' is simply bonkers.

Actually my worries were, by and large, allayed. I had never been to a Select Committee before, though I had watched them on the television. (OK, next question … what happens to a group of media-hungry politicians when you point a TV camera at them?) But I knew that many people thought that (after the House of Lords) they were the best place for finding reasoned and reasonable discussion in our parliamentary process. And so it turned out to be. The discussion took plenty of time (two hours), the MPs had a reasonable knowledge, had done their homework and listened.

So how did it go from our sides? Well, first some of the kids were interviewed. They were brilliant.

If you watched all that footage of the fighting and the
lippiness and the tears on the *Dream School* series, then
this Committee was an antidote. They contributed clearly,
articulately and often movingly – about what had gone wrong
for them at school and what they were hoping to do now. (One
is going round talking to primary schools and hoping to move
into journalism, one is about to do a childcare/youth work
qualification, one is holding three conditional offers for an IT
place at Uni, and so on.) It looks like a total transformation,
which of course it can't be. They must have been like this all
along underneath, but sort of waiting for all this to come out.

Then it was the turn of some of the teachers: the head, plus
me, Alvin Hall, Robert Winston, Jazzie B and David Starkey.

Most of us were singing pretty much from the same hymn
sheet, not too full of doom and gloom about the British
system, a desire to free teachers up a bit, and no passion for the
kind of old-fashioned discipline that people of our age like to
imagine is just what the kids need (and will 'work' … whatever
that means!). And there was plenty of praise for Latin!

Not so Starkey.

He was the only one of us not to turn up to hear the kids
give their evidence. OK, he has obviously hurt his foot, which
is some excuse. But it would in the circumstances have been
wise to have taken the trouble to hear the pupils in action.
For when he later opened his mouth to say what a wild
undisciplined bunch they were, this was dramatically undercut
by what the rest of us had just seen of them when they gave
their evidence.

By and large, he came out with the old Starkey stuff,
interspersed with some silly ad hominem attacks on John
D'Abbro, the Head (who Starkey had somehow failed to see

was in the same boat as the rest of us, in a way, in relation to the TV).

Now Starkey is not stupid, and not everything he says would I disagree with. But his claim that schools which strictly enforce rules on uniform do not have any 'discipline problems' cannot possibly be true. (For a start, 'discipline problems' is not a fixed and objective category ... I shudder to think what got punished at my school).

Overall Starkey is the victim of the kind of tunnel vision that affects many of the successful middle-aged. Because he is a success, he thinks that the kind of schooling he had was the right one. So it might have been – for him. But he has decided not to think of the 'failures' next to whom he sat, still less of the 80% of children who went to the local Secondary Modern. Grammar Schools, excellent as I am sure many of them were and are, always are seen from the point of view of those who got there ... not the rejects. (Not that me and my chums are immune from this kind of glowing nostalgia. When we complain that the kids don't sit down and read as much Latin and Greek during their degrees as we used to do, we tend to forget that 'we' were always unusual, even for Cambridge ... of course we were, else we wouldn't now be Profs there.)

And Starkey could have done his homework better. He lamented the fact that, although he had taken Danielle up to see around Cambridge, and although she was very bright, she still wanted to become a beautician. What a waste, what a lack of ambition, he complained (and what a failure of the education system).

What he had failed to notice was that Danielle has just landed a big part in *EastEnders*. Some ambition there, I suspect.

Exam speak

25 June 2011

I have just finished marking exams (Part IB of the Classical Tripos). That means something like 130 scripts in all. Leaving aside what the candidates will get in the final results table (and that's not decided till next week), I have two immediate reactions.

First, the handwriting. There is something very odd about exams in the twenty-first century, because the kids don't usually, through the academic year, handwrite anything. The good side of this is that you don't recognise the author of any script at all. (In the old days you had marked so many essays in handwriting that you knew exactly whose script you were marking, even if it was formally anonymous.) The bad side is that they are so unused to writing anything by hand that a lot of it borders on the illegible.

Happily the dyslexics are allowed to type their answers, and I found myself longing for the next dyslexic ... or for the day when they were all allowed to type their answers.

By and large, dyslexics apart, this is how it goes. One script in 20, you find 30 sides of crabbed, blotty handwriting. You can just about decipher it, but that probably takes about 5 minutes a side. At a certain point you get so cross that you are tempted to give up. 'Illegibility will be penalised' it says on the papers. Right on, let's penalise.

So what stops you?

Well, in my case, it's partly a family thing (or at least it's put into higher relief that way; the truth is that I have always persevered with this stuff, reluctantly). My son has truly atrocious handwriting. But in Oxford last year some poor examiners persevered with his scrawl, enough to give him a First. For which effort I am truly, truly grateful. So now, when I spend hours on these scripts I can barely read, I think: 'I am not doing it for you, you messy child. I am doing it for your Mum, who wants more than anything that someone will go the extra mile to read your scrawl'. And so I do.

In fact, it can sometimes be very funny prose you end up reading. Exam speak afflicts almost all the candidates, drawing them 'back' to words they have never used … and indeed have not been used in normal writing for generations. I can't count the number of 'aforementioned's I have spotted in these scripts (as in 'the aforementioned legislation'). Not a single one has been penalised by me. But what on earth pushed the students into this archaic speak (how often have any of them used the word before, I wonder)?

Nerves must be the answer, I guess. But it's a very odd idiolect that results.

Comments

As a Classics finalist this year with shamefully spidery handwriting, I must say … THANK YOU! Your patience is deeply comforting.
CJM

AFOREMENTIONED seems to me a very practical word for its purpose. What are the alternatives? 'The widget MENTIONED ABOVE' uses the same number of letters but 'above' suggests a viewpoint other than the author's own, as of someone perusing a document. 'The BEFORE MENTIONED widget' uses one more letter and anyway is hardly idiomatic English. Why the prejudice against (so-called) archaism?

PL

'Saepe memoratum' is one of the Venerable Bede's favourite locutions – usually qualifying a mention of the controversy about the date of Easter.

OLIVER NICHOLSON

To me, the most striking feature of illegibility in handwriting is its gender-specificity. I have sometimes amused myself while marking exams by guessing the gender of the writer from the look of the script, then checking my guess. I can't quote my success rate in this (I'll be a bit more scientific and keep proper records next time), but I think it is close to 100%.

If it's easy to read, and especially if the letters have a nice round form, it's written by a female.

CHRIS JOHNSON

Actually, Prof. Beard, most students write a great deal during the year. Just glance down at the Seeley Library one day in full term and you'll see only one in ten (at most usually) using laptops to make notes. What they may not do is write extended pieces of continuous prose by hand – although some, like Dr RWS at Trinity, force this on their charges' weekly essays.

R STUDENT

I think it's appalling that students are required to handwrite extensive exam scripts in 2011. They never handwrite anything else in the academic year, and wherever life leads them they'll never handwrite anything longer than a Post-it note again.

This seems to me to be a gratuitous piece of meanness only slightly less pointless than demanding they submit their scripts in Caroline minuscule.

CHRIS Y

Why bother to visit the Colosseum?

21 July 2011

OK, it's one of the most memorable buildings in Rome – indeed in Western culture. And the reason I co-wrote a book on it is that I truly believe that its history from ancient gladiatorial arena to nineteenth-century botanical garden is more fascinating than most people realise. It looks absolutely tremendous from the outside. But is it really worth a couple of hours queuing to see the very battered ruins of the interior?

I'm not so sure.

I have just been in Rome for a few days, doing a recce for a new little TV series on ancient Rome (from the point of view of ordinary Romans, not the emperors and generals etc.). I'm not going to give away exactly what we've been seeing – it will ruin the surprise when you watch. (How's that for a tease!) But what has struck me as we have gone round the city of Rome is the mad concentration of tourism.

Everyone wants to see the Colosseum, the Forum and Palatine (all those are on a combined ticket – which you can buy on-line – that's a good tip), the Capitoline museums (on the Campidoglio) and the Vatican.

There are crowds of people, and a dreadful line to get in at almost all times of the day (the later the better is my experience). But go to the wonderful collection of sculpture in the Palazzo Massimo (near the main train station) and you will not have to queue for a minute, and you will find some of the most stunning works of Roman art to have survived (Livia's

Garden Room from Prima Porta is here, for example, and you can't get better than that).

Even fewer people make it to the nearby museum in the Baths of Diocletian (less stunning for art, but some great material on early Rome, a beautiful Michelangelo cloister – and some extraordinary ancient terracotta sculptures, the medium everyone tends to forget).

But the prize for the best least-visited museum must go to the Centrale Montemartini – which houses some of the overspill from the Capitoline collections in a disused power station down the Via Ostiense past the Pyramid. First of all, the juxtaposition of ancient sculpture and industrial machinery is brilliant (like Musée d'Orsay, only better). But it includes some real treasures (the pediment of the Temple of Apollo Sosianus – a first-century BC building which 're-used' a fifth-century BC set of 'original' Greek sculptures; or the tremendous statues from the emperors' pleasure gardens in

Rome). Stunning, and when we were there, we saw two other visitors.

And just outside Rome, there's the port city of Ostia. Now, this is not in truth quite as impressive as Pompeii or Herculaneum in terms of sheer survival. (It was abandoned and gradually covered by sand, not taken out by an earthquake.) But unlike Pompeii, you have the streets more or less to yourself, and you can get a feeling of what it was like to walk through a densely populated Roman town … with series of blocks of flats built in brick. (This was a multiple-occupancy place unlike Pompeii …)

What could be done to entice people away from the 'big few' sites into these other amazing places? They all come fully recommended by me, but do a bit of Googling before you go; the info available on site is not always all it might be. (Amanda Claridge's *Archaeological Guide* covers the city sites well too though it doesn't do Ostia).

Comments

Similar good advice for anyone visiting Florence is not to miss the Museo dell'Opera del Duomo (*ossia*: Museo dell'Opera di Santa Maria del Fiore). Among other unique treasures, it houses Luca della Robbia's singing galleries, Ghiberti's original *Gates of Paradise* reliefs and Michelangelo's last *Pietà*. Everything is well displayed for the serious visitor, the only kind, in my experience, who go there.

PL

My favourite unsung hero in Rome is a five-minute walk from the
Colosseum: the Case Romane del Celio (http://www.caseromane.
it). Some beautiful paintings and you can have the place pretty
much to yourself. (Honourable mention would also go to the
Crypta Balbi and, had the roof not fallen in, the Domus Aurea.) If
you can handle the bus ride, the Villa dei Quintili is a worthwhile
(and quiet) trip to make – come to that, the Villa Adriana isn't
exactly overrun either …

CATERPILLAR

'What could be done to entice people away from the 'big few' sites
into these other amazing places?'

Interestingly, those of us who work at universities other than
Oxford and Cambridge often discuss this question :-) It's a very
similar problem.

PWG

Ara Pacis!!

I used to spend entire days in the quiet glass enclosure.
Occasionally a tour bus would slow down, but few people ever
came in.

IUNIPERA

From El Bulli to Apicius

1 August 2011

I found myself decidedly unmoved by this weekend's obituaries of El Bulli ('the best restaurant in the world'). A friend of mine did make the gastronomic pilgrimage a decade or so ago, and came back full of stories of its brilliance. He had been especially impressed with the way the waiters had held appropriately scented flowers under their noses as they ate particular dishes. My reaction was not 'What brilliant attention to synaesthesia!' but 'How bloody pretentious can you get?'

Try some of his specialities: liquid pea ravioli (that's ravioli shells, filled with pea soup) or flower paper (that's flowers pressed into a sheet of candy floss) or the ball of frozen gorgonzola. All this brings out the culinary philistine in me, or the 'Arts and Crafts, Truth to Materials' approach to cooking. (If God had wanted flowers pressed into a sheet of candy floss … etc. etc. Or why bother to freeze good gorgonzola?)

The husband is with me on this one, but for slightly different reasons. He hates the control exercised by these celebrity cooks; the 'eat what I deign to give you' philosophy. He can't even abide the *amuse-bouches* so beloved of more ordinary pricy restaurants. You know, where the waiter comes up with a little pot of something you hadn't ordered between courses and explains its ingredients to you in a carefully practised French accent. His line is: 'If I'd wanted a 'mousse of dew-picked mushrooms with ginger and cointreau', I'd have asked for it.'

At first sight, all this is much like posh ancient Roman cookery, where again things are not always what they seem. Think, for example, of the dinner party of Petronius' Trimalchio, where half of what the diners eat is not what it seems (quinces masquerading as sea urchins, for example). Or think of one of the signature recipes in Apicius' Roman cook book: 'Casserole of Anchovy without Anchovy' ('at table no one will recognise what they are eating' – and it's actually made of sea nettles and eggs).

But it isn't quite so simple. For while Trimalchio is showing off in an El Bulli type way, Apicius is trying to save money (sea nettles and eggs being, I imagine, cheaper in the Roman market place than bona fide anchovies). Which reminds us of the iron law of cookery, that (William Morris or no William Morris) the whole discipline from top to bottom is riddled with (or rests upon) attempts to turn things into something they are not: chicory into coffee, Quorn into bacon, nuts into cutlets, flour into bread. It's not just the rich turning soup into ravioli parcels: the poor try to make you think sea nettles are anchovy – and all of us prefer a crusty loaf to raw flour, water and yeast. What the El Bullis of this world are doing is only a development of the essentials of cookery (turning 'the raw into the cooked'). So shouldn't I stop the moralising?

And indeed when you actually experience (i.e., eat) one of those really clever confections, it is actually rather exciting. It is easy enough to huff and puff in theory, but when I had a lemon mousse in Washington that looked for all the world like a soft-boiled egg, I was truly enchanted.

'Truth to materials', I guess, doesn't have quite the role in cookery as it does in architecture.

Comments

Oh joy, I can finally be as pretentious as I like, knowing full well I'll
be outdone by El Bulli. Years ago, at La Côte St-Jacques in Joigny
(Burgundy) – then a mere 2-star; now 3 stars – my partner and I
had the waiters remove an elaborate flower arrangement from
a nearby table as its perfume interfered with our tasting the
foie gras. Thank heavens they obliged rather than holding the
offending blooms under our noses.

JUDITH WEINGARTEN

Since the dawn of time, there have been only two truly great
cookery books.
1. Edouard de Pomiane, *La cuisine en dix minutes*.
2. Caroline Blackwood and Anna Haycraft, *Darling, You
   Shouldn't Have Gone To So Much Trouble*.

RICHARD BARON

A plea for Apicius: trying to cook meals from this is tremendously
illuminating. Of course, the food will never be quite 'right', but
it may be delicious. The strangeness and complexity of flavours
provide an immediate (and unexpected) awareness of the
sophistication and irretrievably remote complexity of another
world. (If you're too squeamish for dormice or garum, try the dates:
Apicius recipe no. 296)

JH

I am reminded of the British Library café. I felt rather short-
changed when 'avocado and celeriac remoulade with harissa

dressing on a white bloomer' turned out to be a coleslaw sandwich.

LIZ C

If you want to explore Apicius' recipes, try C. Grocock and S. Grainger (eds), Apicius: A Critical Edition with an Introduction and English Translation *(Prospect Books, 2006).*

The Cambridge Chancellor election – in 1847

11 August 2011

I haven't been to the Manuscripts Room of the University Library for a year of so (chance would be a fine thing). So I hadn't caught up with the new policing regime that I found when I showed up there this week: you now have to sign in on a separate admissions list, and you aren't allowed to take in even the small-size bags that are allowed into the rest of the Library; instead you have to leave it in a locker outside ... and you end up having to get the key back (because, wisely maybe, they don't trust you to keep the key on your person) every time you want to get 25p to buy a new pencil, or whatever.

I'm sure that this is all very sensible, and a good way of protecting the collection. But it does have a nasty way of criminalising you, and of raising the uncomfortable possibility that you and every other reader in the room might be liable to snitch some precious document as soon as anyone's back might be turned. (I wonder how many people it pushes to crime, at the same time as it makes it harder for them.)

Anyway, I was not to be put off, as I was there on the search of more things about the history of the Fitzwilliam Museum. One thing I wanted to get to the bottom of was the celebrations in 1842 in honour of the new chancellor, the Duke of Northumberland, part of which took place in the Museum before the building had even been finished. Just how unfinished, I wondered.

One likely-looking document was catalogued as the description of the election and installation of about five new Chancellors over the course of the nineteenth century, a manuscript written by eager, obsessive and rather smart nineteenth-century bureaucrats, keen to pass on the proceedings to their successors.

It turned out not to have anything to help me about the state of the Fitzwilliam in 1842, but it had lots of juicy stuff about the election of 1847– which turned out to have quite a lot in common with the election we are to have in October.

As I vaguely recollected (but it was brought vividly to life by this carefully written account), the establishment candidate in 1847 was Prince Albert – but, against him, the awkward squad, largely based in St John's, put up a rival in the shape of the Earl of Powis (a truly awful Tory, MP for Ludlow and dyed-in-the-wool opponent of the 1832 Reform Act).

After a bit of a wobble the Prince did not actually withdraw and went through with a lively election, which offers a load of tips for the supporters of the rival candidates this time round … including organising committees, and specially chartered trains from London to bring the voters in. (One of the things that the Prince's opponents worried about was that he would try to Germanise the University – another was that the backdoor connection between University and crown was a bit unseemly.)

It appears to have been a spirited fight, with Albert winning comfortably but not by a huge majority. The anonymous bureaucrat of my document then lavishes his pen on the dinner held at the palace to celebrate the successful election (silver knives and forks for the first course, he insists, gold for the dessert). Apparently the Earl of Powis was invited but couldn't come.

Which all makes you wonder about how the victory of one of our four candidates – Lord Sainsbury, the Mill Road grocer, Brian Blessed and Michael Mansfield – might be celebrated in October. Not so extravagantly, I guess, but I'll let you know.

Comments

They were right about the Prince Consort: he did interfere, at least on one occasion I know of. In 1860 he pushed for the appointment of Charles Kingsley as Regius Professor of History – largely on the basis of his historical novels, and against the wishes of the academic historians.

MARION DIAMOND

Don't feel criminalised. These sound like sensible and usual precautions around rare materials. Years ago, when a graduate student at Cambridge, I wished to use a very rare Chaucer MS. I won't say which college it belonged to. I was left alone with it and could have eaten a three-course meal on top of it or removed some choice pages. When I finished, I looked for someone to give it to. I wandered aimlessly around the college and finally the porter telephoned someone, of importance I supposed, and I turned it over. I still shudder when I think of this carelessness.

ERIKA

The Africa Museum in Brussels – and David Starkey

14 August 2011

Even if you haven't read Adam Hochschild's *King Leopold's Ghost*, it's hard not to have picked up the point that Belgian rule in the Congo was terrible even by the usual standards of European colonialism in Africa. That said, I've always had a soft spot for the Royal Museum of Central Africa, just outside Brussels. (and it has an honoured place on of my list of favourite but little-known museums).

I first visited this museum (in Tervuren, a quick tram ride from central Brussels) almost ten years ago, with the daughter when she was doing a school project on the Congo. Then it was in its pristine state: it was a museum of itself, 'celebrating' the Belgian 'achievement' against the African 'savages'. Pride of place went to the statues in the front hall, large gilded

personifications of kindly Belgium bringing peace, prosperity
and civilisation to the grateful Congolese – but the early
nineteenth-century display of colonial memorabilia told a
similar story. Stanley emerged as almost as much of a hero as
Leopold, and the Heart of Darkness was nowhere to be seen.

A few years later we went again, and things were on the
move – for the worse, I couldn't help feeling. There were
glimpses of post-colonial political correctness appearing in the
galleries, which, understandable as they were, were so against
the grain of the collection and its display (the whole thing had
been put together under the auspices of Leopold himself, for
heaven's sake) that they risked looking faintly silly. They were
in fact a bit like the new wave at the Natural History Museum
in London, with its pious little notices about how we wouldn't
hunt and stuff wild animals these days. It seemed to me that it
would have just been better to leave the whole thing as it was
and let us see what the colonial vision was like straight, and
allow us to make our own minds up.

Anyway, I went back (with the husband and the son) this
weekend and was prepared for the worst: I fully expected
computer screens and interactive push buttons … 'The Belgian
intervention in the Congo was: (a) good or (b) bad)', with a
serious computerised ticking off to anyone stupid enough to
press button (a).

Actually, it turned out to be a nice surprise. For quite a
lot of the early twentieth-century display had been rather
carefully, and self-awarely, restored. True, this was mostly
in the natural history parts of the museum (despite the
difficulties South Kensington seems to have, it is actually
rather easier to come to terms with the colonial treatment of
elephants than the colonial treatment of human beings). But
even in the historical sections, a good deal of the post-colonial

points were being made by adding sharp twenty-first-century responses to the traditional displays. There was, for example, a great photographic exhibition contrasting pictures taken in the Congo under Belgian rule with pictures taken now. In fact, this was part of a project that tried to gather contemporary Congolese reactions to old colonial photos – something the daughter is currently wanting to do in South Sudan.

All the same, the most dramatic impact in the museum is still the front hall, with those gilded statues of Belgian beneficence to the benighted natives (even if some of them are now awkwardly – or conveniently – hidden behind the coat lockers). What strikes me, looking at these, is not the fact that some of the Belgian administration (and for 'Belgian' you could read 'British') must have been well aware that paternalism was a convenient cover for exploitation. I am sure that was sometimes the case; but more often the Belgian bourgeoisie must have turned up to this Museum and genuinely felt that it was a testament to their country's good works.

Which is to say that the interesting historical question (and one that the decor of the Brussels Museum raises emphatically) is not whether colonialism/empire was good or bad; but how we can start to understand how it seemed morally good to so many ordinary, decent Western people? Self-interest isn't a good enough answer. But there is an unimaginable leap of historical empathy here.

Those were the thoughts on the tram back to the hotel, where we caught up with the new David Starkey row, which was not entirely unconnected. If I have got the story right, Starkey was in trouble for saying (in one of those post-riots post-mortems) that if you heard the Tottenham MP David Lammy on the radio you would think he was white.

Starkey seems to have thought this somehow to Lammy's (or
the country's) discredit, whereas I felt that it was probably
something to celebrate that you couldn't tell a black from
a white voice on Radio 4 (or alternatively that, as always in
Britain, it was class not race that was audible).

Lammy was, to start with, pretty restrained in his reply, but
eventually came out with words to the effect of 'Starkey should
stick to sounding off about the Tudors'. The objections to
this were obvious. Starkey might be a rather undistinguished
example of the genre – but the Brussels Museum makes
the powerful case that we DO need historians thinking and
speaking about exactly these issues of race and ideology.

Comments

Mary, I think your post invites this question: just how much nasty
drivel does somebody have to speak before the focus of your
response shifts from 'nobody should tell a historian to shut up'
to 'historians shouldn't talk nonsense' (nonsense with potential
consequences)?
RICHARD

Richard, I never said 'nobody should tell a historian to shut
up', I said that just because Starkey's specialist subject is the
Elizabethans is not a good reason to shut him up.

Just for the sake of completeness, this is what D Lammy said:
'Yes, I have now seen what he [sc. Starkey] said. His views are
irrelevant – he's a Tudor historian talking about contemporary
urban unrest.'

I would like to see Starkey's views well and truly quashed … but we have to quash them for the right reasons.

As one of my Oxford mates said to me, the worst thing that Starkey has done is to have given us a sense of moral certitude in opposition to him.

MARY BEARD

As a historian, Beard should be consulting the evidence before she writes her blog.

LIZX

Liz, If 'Beard' followed your rather rigid prescriptions, she might be writing good history, but it wouldn't be a very entertaining blog.

LL

Starkey's was a complex point, easily misinterpreted (as we have seen), and it certainly does not deserve to be 'quashed', which is a surprising choice of word from someone who claims to be holding out for free speech. I dare say what makes him 'undistinguished' in your eyes is his refusal to kowtow to the liberal orthodoxies of the quad and court. Or maybe it is just the gentle envy of one media don for another with a bigger telly contract.

HAMPSTEAD OWL

Why does the Manneken Pis?

18 August 2011

The icon of Brussels is (to judge from the souvenir shops at least) the bronze fountain/statue of the little boy pissing, the Manneken Pis. It is an image that, in Brussels, goes back to the seventeenth century; but the idea of a fountain spouting water as if it was peeing goes back at least to the Romans, and probably before. It's not a hugely imaginative idea.

Anyway, you can now buy battalions of this little guy, most made I guess in China. (A few blazon 'Made in Belgium', but most are not homegrown – has anyone ever gone to one of these Chinese factories where miniature images of the great monuments of the West are churned out?) And if you don't fancy a key-ring, you can buy him in chocolate, or see him in a more than life-size pretend-chocolate model. Every tour group is brought to admire.

My question was: why has *this* become the icon of
Belgium? Most cities have a much more visible symbol (Big
Ben, the Parthenon, the Eiffel Tower), but this little boy is
barely a metre tall and in what would have been a back street,
if it hadn't been for him. He is supposed to go back to the early
seventeenth century (stolen and broken up in the nineteenth,
and remade from a mould of the pieces), and there are all
kinds of urban legends about what he might stand for. The one
I was told years ago was that he was a lost rich child, whose
father vowed a statue of him doing whatever he was doing if
and when he was found. But there are plenty of others. I rather
like the idea that it reminds us of the brave kids of Brussels
who ensured their city's victory by pissing on the enemy from
trees.

What I hadn't realised till we went last week was that he
also had a wardrobe.

Kept in the Musée de la Ville de Bruxelles are the many
and varied costumes he has been presented with by local and
visiting delegations. Where these are made, heaven knows …
but I have never seen the little chap dressed up.

Anyway, we couldn't resist going to see his kit when we
were there last weekend. And as we going out of the Museum
we couldn't help notice some packs of what looked like repro
1950s' postcards. These confirmed the sense of wonder –
because they foregrounded the sexuality of the image that
most modern renderings would ostensibly disavow. OK,
they were sexualised only at one remove, but sexualised
nevertheless. The repeated joke (and it came in various forms)
was the one about the middle-aged lady who sees the statue of
the little boy and suddenly gets horny … to the distress of her
middle-aged husband, who sees that he is in for an energetic
night.

You couldn't sell these now. Or could you? And in what
form? We imagined that we were buying repros of historic
souvenirs. But getting them out on the train back home, they
looked more like the real thing. There was nothing printed on
the back about what they were copying, and the edges were
decidedly yellow. Were they actually still flogging old stock?

And still no one had quite explained why this pissing
toddler was the icon of the city. Is it really just, as the
guidebooks would claim, an encapsulation of the 'irreverent
spirit' of Brussels … a kind of Tintin *avant la lettre*?

Comments

One of the most often repeated stories about Manneken Pis is that
he saved Brussels. As the story goes, a plot to destroy the city was
forged, explosive or incendiary devices left in place and a primer
set alight in order to let the terrorists flee. But the young man
came along and extinguished the primer, thus saving the city. The
other speaks of a very young duke taken on a battlefield where he
came out of his bed at a time when the battle was going badly for
his forces, the sight of him pissing toward his enemies giving heart
to his men, who went on to win the fight.

In any case, a version of the statue has been in the city since
at least 1388. It has been part of the history of the city for so long
that it became a symbol of resistance, especially after Brussels's
siege by Louis XIV's armies, during which the statue was hidden
and after which the inscription 'In petra exaltavit me, et nunc
exaltavi caput meum super inimicos meos' was engraved. As for
the clothes, it seems it became a tradition just after the siege

when the Spanish governor-general Maximilien-Emmanuel de Bavière gave its first set of clothes to the boy.

Signed: A Classical-period historian and digital humanist living on top of the highest tower in the less than fashionable area just behind the Covent Garden in Brussels. (Yes, culture and science may bloom in the most unexpected areas.)

PASCAL LEMAIRE

Fed up with the REF ... and what about the babies?

1 September 2011

In case you don't know, the 'REF' (the 'Research Excellence Framework', which sounds like the higher education equivalent of a 'record of achievement') is the new version of the 'RAE' (the 'Research Assessment Exercise', which was at least honest enough to admit that it was judgemental ... more like the old 'school report'). It is the process by which the government evaluates the research 'output' of university departments (and indeed of the individual academics within those departments) and then distributed (or not) money accordingly.

No surprise that I have little sympathy with this process. It's not that I think university academics should not be in some form accountable to those who (in large part, but not wholly) pay for them. But this process is overall a block on good, imaginative research in the humanities (and maybe in the sciences too). It dominates the thinking of university administrators. Try appointing someone to a university job who – whatever good reason – doesn't look as if they are going to have a 'robust' submission (that is new uni speak even among the dreaming spires) for the REF. And it sets a load of ingenious people off on the chase of clever ways to come out on top ... so that the government can thrash us all, or rather some of us, again. Divide and rule, it used to be called.

No department wants to be a three-star (or whatever it will be called this time), else some slasher VC will come in and slash them (or, if they are VERY LUCKY INDEED, will give them extra research leave, and two new super-star colleagues (no teaching duties) so they can do better next time … dream on).

I realise, of course, that many of my own colleagues have done valiant jobs and spent weeks of their life in evaluating all this research activity in past assessment exercises, to ensure that the process is still a peer review, not some metric exercise – which would reward the popular and bad (and to be fair the popular and good) at the expense of the brilliant and unfashionable. (A bit like Cambridge University Library thinking you can judge the value of a periodical on the basis of how many times it has been borrowed.) Don't think I'm ungrateful to them. But all the same, I don't like the system.

Today, though, it isn't the higher principles, or 'the system', that are annoying me. It is what the REF has done to my summer.

Now I haven't been research-inactive over the last few years; indeed I have written a lot, had quite a bit of 'impact' (another bit of uni new speak) and I have given two big series of lectures in the states (Sathers and Mellons) which took a hell of a lot of work to do, which other people would long to give and which I am dying to write up. What I wanted to do this summer was to get down to Roman Laughter (the Sather topic) and get it pretty well finished … but hang on.

I have to submit four 'outputs' published between 2008 and the end of 2013. My Pompeii book is an obvious one, as is a big article about to come out on nineteenth-century travel to Pompeii. After that I have a variety of things, including a new article in an exhibition catalogue on the secret cabinet in the Naples Museum, a total rewrite of a piece on 'Oriental Cults' I did a few years ago (this is effectively a new paper, but will it count?), some stuff on Roman Britain in the late nineteenth century, plus a Darwin lecture on Risk … and a paper on Samuel Butler that didn't actually appear till 2008, although the title page is dated 2007 etc. etc.

What I ought to have done this summer was get down and conquer my Laughter book. That would have made the most intellectual sense, and it would have been best for the subject, and for me. But I sat down and thought, hell – if I get to it now, it still might not come out by the end of 2013, there might be all kinds of hold-ups, and the University of California Press doesn't quite get the REF issue …

What I need to be safe, I thought, is another sure-fire article. So I wrote an article on the history of the Fitzwilliam Classical Collection, which I have enjoyed (a lot actually), and which I had promised … but in the end I only really did it because of the damn REF, when I should have spent the summer on Laughter.

So if anyone ever tells you that the REF doesn't skew people's research plans, I for one can tell you that it does.

Then, just as I was reflecting gloomily on this subject, I was told that the most recent consultative document for the rules for the REF proposes normally giving women who have had kids no allowance in the evaluation unless they have had more than 14 months' maternity leave in the 5 years. (For most of us, who can't afford unpaid maternity leave, that would mean having had 3 kids in 5 years.) The idea is supposed to be that you have your maternity leave and then are back to normal. (An alternative and, in my view, much better suggestion would be to credit women with an output for each baby … so one child born in the period and you would only need 3 outputs, 2 and you would only need 2.)

This idea of not recognising the research effects of young babies is surely mad. I have tried writing articles with two kids under three. It isn't about just the official maternity leave. What you need to write good articles and books in my subjects is uninterrupted thinking time. So what blights your productivity for a good while are the trips backward and forwards to feed the baby, the fact that you can't go to all those seminars you used to go to (people forget about you and what you might be doing) – and you certainly can't go to conferences (unless you fancy sitting in the bog and expressing the milk for what seems like hours on end, while everyone else is networking).

If there had been a REF on these terms in the mid-1980s, I would have been a casualty (i.e., I would have been a failure) … and I probably would have left the University and got another job. Twenty years on (and it takes 20 years), I am confident enough to say that that would have been a loss.

Where are our equal opps people when we need them?

Comments

I'm going to get lynched for saying this, but …

I have two kids aged three and under. I breast-fed them both (still feeding the youngest) up to a year or so. I am a senior academic at a top university in the UK. I took a year off on maternity leave with each. One of them has woken up every 2.5 hours through the night since he was born.

And I'm scratching my head at what to put in to the REF (my manager has just asked for preliminary suggestions) as I have 14 things which count, and more in the pipeline.

I planned ahead.

And quite frankly, I'm narked that my hard work on top of my leave (and difficult pregnancies, births and recovery) isn't going to be rewarded, and that nothing takes into consideration my high level of high-class output. No, I do not want my input to be reduced to two items! Judge me on my real performance!

I could do with some sleep, though.

MONKEYBEAR5000

What Tony Blair should have written to Saif Gaddafi

4 September 2011

According to this morning's papers, Tony Blair, who had been sent a chunk of Saif Gaddafi's thesis, wrote back to him thanking him for showing him his 'interesting thesis' and giving him a few examples that might help his research (ill-fated research, as it turned out, in more ways than one). This has apparently been revealed in documents that have turned up in Tripoli, and a Blair spokesperson has explained that (although the letter was signed by TB) he hadn't actually read the thesis and the whole thing had been drafted by 'officials'.

Let's assume two things. One (this is fairly likely): that Saif had written to Blair asking him to read his work and also asking for a bit of help. Two (rather less likely – but you never know): that any graduate student who wrote to Number 10 asking for some help with their thesis would get the backroom boys and girls finding them some good examples for their doctorate.

On those assumptions, my reaction is that Blair and his team hadn't learned the lesson that most academics quickly learn, who tend to be deluged with requests by people (from novelists and doctoral students to primary school kids writing a project) asking them to read their work, and/or to give a bibliography, or to 'tell me what you know about'.

It's always a tricky one, but you begin to get a nose for a right answer.

You are weighing up (in my case at least) two
considerations that pull in very different ways. On the one
hand, I think that I have a duty to the subject and to helping
people find out about it. If a kid who seems to have got
enthused about ancient Greece and wants a bit of advice about
how to take that further, surely you should help. At the same
time, if a Masters or doctoral student at some other university
is working on a subject that is part of your 'territory', then I
think that there is a presumption that you should be interested
in them and give a hand (and I think I have a pretty good
record at that).

But if I read everything I was asked to, and gave a full
bibliography to everyone who emailed in for one, I wouldn't
have any time for any of my own work at all. And just
occasionally I get the feeling that I am being a bit 'used' –
whether to compensate for someone who is not doing their
supervisory job elsewhere (and whose university is taking the
fat fee) or to be an innocent weapon in some battle between
a student and their long suffering supervisor ('Mary Beard
said … '), or just to save the person's time of half-an-hour
Googling. And sometimes I get the feeling that the innocent
inquirer has actually written round to half the Classical world
asking for a bibliography on gladiators or whatever. (Those I
guess are the ones who can't be bothered to send an email to
thank you, even though they could be bothered to email you to
ask you the question.)

So I have a variety of strategies, while still trying to be
helpful. I sometimes ask how many people have they sent
the 'I am doing a project on Roman London … ' email to.
Sometimes I suggest they start with their own teacher, then
come to me. Sometimes I ask what they have already done
to find out about the subject. This doesn't work badly, and

actually I have made some good friends this way. As I say, you get a nose for it, and for how to help those who need/deserve the help – while not being a complete mug and spending an hour assembling the information that they could have done themselves. The same goes with requests for how to visit Pompeii … it's great when you have some feedback and people tell you about how it worked (or not); when you give a load of advice about places, sites, transport and hotels, and you don't even get an acknowledgement, AAGGGHHH.

So what should Blair have done? Well, my hunch is that he should have written back, suggesting that Saif's supervisor at LSE was the best resource on this. (He or his staff ought to have wanted to get a scent if there was a problem here – there clearly was.) Anyway, sending off some half-relevant example never really helps anyone; that's not what a PhD is about really.

And he (or his staff) should NEVER have sort of implied that he had read the work sent in by Saif when he hadn't.

Any academic would have told him that trouble always comes that way – as indeed it has in this case.

Comments

I'm pretty sure that the reason he showed it to Blair was that he expected the Prime Minister to call up the LSE and quietly tell them that they'd better give him a PhD or else …

After all, isn't that the way things were done in Libya?

MARKS

Just as amusing as requests for assistance are supposed answers to long-standing problems, discoveries of the key to the Universe, claims of royal blood and entitlement to the kingdom and so on.

Littlewood, in *A Mathematician's Miscellany* (p. 43 of the 1953 edition), tells the following story:

Landau kept a printed form for dealing with proofs of Fermat's last theorem. 'On page blank, lines blank to blank, you will find there is a mistake.' (Finding the mistake fell to the Privat Dozent.)

RICHARD BARON

Nisi dominus frustra: why ditch a motto?

16 September 2011

Melbourn Village College – not far from Cambridge – has
decided to ditch its Latin motto: 'Nisi dominus frustra'. And
I guess you can see why. It's a contraction of the first line
of Psalm 127, 'Unless the Lord builds the house, those who
build it labour in vain' ... so you might translate the three
Latin words of the motto something like 'Without the Lord,
frustration', I guess. A touch pious you might think, and
a bit Judaeo-Christian. But I can't see that any world faith
could seriously disagree and, anyway, it's served the city of
Edinburgh well enough for the last few hundred years.

They have replaced it (after a student vote, it seems) with
what sounds to me more like an advertising jingle: 'Inspiring
Minds' (which is bound to look 'so 2011' in a few years time
that it too will soon be ditched). According to the Acting
Principal, they wanted a motto that was more relevant to the
students. In the current economic climate, Latin was 'largely
irrelevant' in helping the students find work.

Never mind the dodgy logic and/or facts here. (Every study
I have seen suggests that Latin has a rather good track record
in employment – but even if it didn't, we surely don't think that
school is all about jobs: what about EDUCATION?) More to
the point is the question of what we think mottoes are for.

I've never been much of a fan of obscuring stupid ideas
under a veil of Latin (as if translating stupidity into a 'dead'
language suddenly made it clever). But I do think mottoes are
best when they are a bit mystical, a tiny bit puzzling (which

is presumably why Latin mottoes are a favourite of football clubs). I would have thought that enterprising teaching could easily use 'Nisi dominus frustra' to make something that was fascinating and life-enhancing for the kids. It would take you, for a start, into the Psalms (which, Judaeo-Christian or not, are an important part of world culture), and it would take you to the history of Edinburgh (which, as a city, wouldn't be too bad a role model for a school).

But the real problem is that – to judge from its website – Melbourn Village College doesn't actually teach Latin, which must be one reason why the students found the phrase irrelevant. (To be fair, they have a good range of Modern Languages and most students study two, at least for a bit; which must make the school a bit of a beacon in that department.)

I wonder if any of the teachers explained the motto and its history to the kids before they voted to ditch it. And I wonder if the Acting Principal considered the possibility of dealing with the apparent irrelevance by (re-)introducing Latin into the curriculum.

That might have opened up even more exciting educational horizons to their students.

Comments

Once, on an OFSTED inspection, a pupil told me that he hadn't a clue what the school motto meant and that if they'd wanted him to know they wouldn't have written it in a foreign language. (It was in Latin.)

GEOFFREY WALKER

I must say a motto that suggests you have to believe in the Lord in order for your labours to be fruitful is not a motto I would want for myself or my child's school. Very depressing if you are not of the tribe.

STROPPY AUTHOR

But the motto and the full text it's extracted from say nothing about believing in the Lord; only about collaborating with Him. A belief in His existence is, of course, implied. But that's no reason for an atheist to take offence. Each to his own metaphysical assumptions.

PL

Our school motto was 'Fidei coticula crux' (it was run by a Catholic teaching order). But not even the Latin masters knew what it meant. The sticking point was 'coticula'. Someone once suggested that it meant 'touchstone', which I believe was correct, but as no one knew what a touchstone was, it didn't help much.

Now, long after the event, I suppose it means 'The Cross is the test of faith', which is a good religious motto, but doesn't seem appropriate to a school that I rather enjoyed than otherwise.

But what is a motto for? Oxford's 'Dominus Illuminatio mea' was probably meaningful when invented: 'The Lord enlightens my mind' or some such; especially if you think of Grosseteste discoursing on light, but nowadays rather begs the question of which Dominus, and whether there is a Dominus at all.

DAVID KIRWAN

How about a return *ad fontes* with:
אוש אל היהו מא
(if that's correct)?

PL

Nisi Dominus frustra is the motto of St John's College, University of Sydney. As acting Rector, after nights of riotous student behaviour, I often fantasised about reducing the motto to FRUSTRA.

CF

Filming: the boot on the other foot

19 September 2011

When I was curator of the Museum of Classical Archaeology in Cambridge, I used to be terribly ambivalent about film crews wanting to come and use the Museum as a location. (It's a great one, by the way.) On the one hand, it was wonderful publicity for what we had to offer: a free advert, really. On the other, it was always a total pain in the neck. The crew would turn up with mind-boggling amounts of equipment, they completely disrupted the place for any other visitor – and they always, just always, went on for longer than they said they would. I tried adding on penalty payments for every 15 minutes over the agreed time, but even that didn't work (though it did bring in more cash).

Now the boot is on the other foot. I'm in Italy filming a documentary series on ancient Rome, and I have become one of those villains I used to find so infuriating – with all that stuff, getting in everyone's way and sometimes, I confess, going on too long. A salutary lesson, I guess. I have come to see why it is so hard to be a 'well-behaved' film crew.

The timing really is extremely tight and disconcertingly unpredictable. Even if you have recce'd every location pretty carefully, you still can't be prepared for everything: the fact that it is a rainy day and very dark and you have to light the place, or a man is digging up the road with a pneumatic drill right outside (and it takes half an hour to persuade him just to take a five-minute break), or the air force has chosen to practise its

tricks overhead, or your presenter (that's me) keeps fluffing her lines.

I don't really mean 'lines', as there is isn't a written script as such. We know the basic points we want to make at each location, but I do it extempore to camera each time.

You couldn't really do otherwise if you want to make it fresh and good and well targeted. Actually being in the place suggests new connections and new emphases in what you should be saying. But it's horribly easy to get it wrong first time, or even second time … not to say third.

Sometimes that's a matter of tone (too breezy, or not breezy enough). Sometimes it's a question of just getting bogged down in some not very relevant detail – or realising that you just forgot the wonderful example that you meant to put in. Sometimes you have to take 15 minutes to check a fact that you hadn't realised you needed. I'm travelling with a mini reference library, plus access to JSTOR in the evening – but thank God for Google on a smartphone during the day, which is great when you have had a sudden crisis of confidence about the exact meaning of a Latin word (the brilliant Perseus website gives you Lewis and Short's Latin Dictionary on-line) or suddenly blank on the date of death of Trajan. (No, I don't trust Wiki!)

Making a slip in a lecture is bad enough, but you can always put it right the next time – you can even make it slightly endearing on the 'Homer nods' principle. If you make an error in front of a few million (let's hope) viewers, that's more seriously humiliating, to say the least. (And just think of the number of emails you'd get.)

So it's hardly surprising that you tend to run over time. OK, you could just double the time you thought you would need at each location, but that would end you up with big gaps, and wasted time and money … and you'd probably annoy people just as much, for different reasons.

And it's hardly surprising that it's as exhausting as it is adrenalin-generating. We regularly leave the hotel at 7.30 in the morning and get back at 7.30 at night, before a couple of hours final prep for the next day has to be done (by me), and hitches with equipment, locations, permissions sorted out and tomorrow's shots planned (by the others).

It all makes me feel a tiny bit guilty about how fierce I was with the hapless, over-running film crews in our Museum.

Comments

I'm sure you are doing a brilliant job, but the man with the road
drill has my sympathy. When we lived in the Cotswolds, trying
to get on with some forestry, we were interrupted by the Beeb's
natural history unit doing a programme on newts. No prior
contact or agreement. We were chain-sawing 300 yards away and
suddenly the crew started waving and shouting 'Shhh ...' It was
slightly inane.

PETER WOOD

As a TV director, I read this with great interest – and Mary's got
the day in the life of a film crew pretty much spot-on. Added to
the list of distractions and delays she describes, if you throw into
the mix autograph hunters / well-meaning well-wishers / people
who absolutely have to wave at the camera (meaning a retake) /
a presenter who absolutely has to have their sushi from a certain
place the other side of the city and any number of other things
that could occur, it's rare that a day can go exactly to schedule, no
matter how well prepared and professional a crew is. (Incidentally
– the only people in the country who were happy about the
volcanic ash cloud last year were sound recordists; with no planes
overhead it was quite incredible how much smoother a day's
filming went!)

A DIRECTOR

AD VS. CE

26 September 2011

Let's get this quite straight: the BBC has not banned the use of BC and AD, in favour of the religiously neutral BCE and CE. Though that is what a quick glance at a few of this week's newspapers would suggest.

'The Corporation has replaced the familiar 'Anno Domini' (the year of Our Lord) and 'Before Christ' with the obscure terms 'Common Era' and 'Before Common Era' intoned the *Daily Mail*, while giving a hearty pat on the back to the almost unknown medieval monk, Dionysius Exiguus ('Little Dennis'), who invented the BC/AD system. If some people find the BCE/CE terminology a bit obscure, that is nothing compared with the obscurity of Dionysius Exiguus – who has been enjoying a totally unexpected five minutes of fame.

No, the BBC hasn't banned BC and AD. So far as I can see, various departments within the organisation have advised that BCE and CE may sometimes be more appropriate for a multicultural/multi-faith audience. It has done not much more than draw the issue to the attention of its editorial staff.

I'm actually surprised that it needed much drawing. In my world CE and BCE have been around for years, and often used instead of BC and AD. I would say that some 50% of academic articles in Ancient History now use CE and BCE, more in the USA. And it hasn't brought the Christian church down – and certainly not in America.

The issues here are both clear and tricky. First BC and AD are certainly totally embedded in a Christian world view,

though that may be conveniently and usefully concealed
beneath the standard abbreviations. In fact, Dionysius did
not invent the shorthand BC and AD in the shortened form,
he invented the whole principle of arranging time around the
birth of Jesus Christ.

Imagine if every newsreader spelled it out in full 'England's
World cup victory, in the year of our Lord 1966....' or whatever.
Then there really would be howls of protest, some of them
from the very same people who are now objecting to the
rumoured demise of BC and AD.

There is no doubt that this is a Christian system. The
problem is that the CE/BCE replacement doesn't exactly
un-Christianise it. Dionysius was super-successful to the
extent that in most circumstances in the West it is now
impossible to imagine unpicking the Christian calendar.
(Geologists have done it up to a point with BP, 'Before Present'
– because with the time periods they are dealing with the line
drawn 2,000 years ago doesn't matter very much.) So you
might say 'Why Bother?' ... wouldn't it just be better to make
people a bit more aware of the Christian framework built into
our calendar?

My particular problem with CE and BCE is rather different
though. It's an oral one. If you lecture, then BC and AD are
great, as it is so easy for your audience to 'hear' the difference.
If you use CE and BCE when you are speaking, you are always
having to over-enunciate to make sure they get the point and
the difference. And even then, many a hapless undergraduate
fails to register, and gets Nero before Julius Caesar.

So if there is a reason that the BBC should generally stick
to the old usage, for me it is that it is simply easier to 'hear'.
Which is quite different from the BBC bashing, 'I-don't-
pay-my-licence-fee-to-have-the-Lefty-BBC undermine-

Christianity' kind of drivel that has come flooding out, even from people who should know better – like Boris Johnson.

Comments

As someone who's hopeless at dates, I'd prefer more inexactitude. So, how about something like this: NSLA – not so long ago, AGWS – a good while since, Y – yonks, AH – ancient history, BTA – before the Ark.

MICHAEL BULLEY

I once suggested DE, which stands for 'Dennis's Era', as the guy who established the number of years after Christ's birth was called Dennis. That seems to me to leave the religion more out of it, and name the guy who set up the system.

SW FOSKA

The whole point of political correctness is to make people think, get them out of the cultural groove for a moment. I'd hold my hand up as a silly leftie, because I think slightly outrageous proposals do move the debate on, making certain default presuppositions visible and up for argument. I'm currently reading a very silly German translation of the Bible (*Bibel in Gerechte Sprache*), which puts back women everywhere, e.g. 'Propheten and Prophetinnen' where we'd normally just read 'prophets'. I'm doubtful about how many female prophets there were (yes, some, but in every situation??), but when it comes to disciples of Jesus, it's great to see 'die Jünger und Jüngerinnen', because the women who followed Jesus are made so often invisible in the Gospels. So I'm all for that kind of silliness.

NICK JOWETT

May I quote (without permission) from David Abulafia in the preface to his history of the Mediterranean *The Great Sea*: 'Those who are uncomfortable with 'Before Christ' and 'Anno Domini' are free to decide that BC and AD stand for some other combination of words, such as 'Backward chronology' and 'Accepted date'.'

By the way, 'Weedy Dionysius' (a little joke courtesy of an RC priest I used to know) got it wrong, and the best date for the birth of Jesus of Nazareth is in the range 8–6 BC, making him perhaps the only person in history to have been born at the age of minus 8, or at any rate minus 6. At any rate, if you follow Matthew, then he had to be born before Herod the Great died in 4 BC(E).

DAVID KIRWAN

First-year Ancient History at Newnham. What do we do?

19 October 2011

Every year one of my favourite bits of teaching is with my Newnham first-year students (technically, I mean, Part 1A – because a few of them have already done our Prelim course, designed for those without A level Latin, or equivalent, and so are in their second year at Cambridge). First-year teaching is fun (and hard) because you are trying to educate (in the technical sense: i.e., not cram) a highly intelligent group of students, but they are being asked to make a very quick transition between school and university. To put it crudely, and a bit unfairly to A levels, they have quickly to become independent learners (with support and guidance); they have to discover what it is to explore a historical topic without knowing that there is a checklist of criteria whose boxes they have to tick in order to get a first, 2.1 or whatever; and they have to discover that intellectual inquiry is open-ended, exciting, difficult if you do it well, and that it matters.

So what do I get them to do for their first piece of supervision (i.e., tutorial) work?

Well, 15 years ago, I used just to set a 'straight' essay … something like a 'How useful is the evidence of Lysias 1 for the position of women in Classical Athens?', appending a bibliography which gave them (albeit indirectly) the answer. There were, in fact, some good lessons here. Lysias 1 – a speech given c. 400 BC about the murder of a certain Erastosthenes, allegedly killed after being caught *in flagrante* with another man's wife – was a first-year set text. And in the process of writing the essay they learned a lot about it and about the position of women in Classical Athens. Not bad.

But they didn't learn much about exploring for themselves (they followed the bibliography I had given, rather over-dutifully, despite exhortations to follow up other stuff they came across), and they didn't learn much about the overall picture. Ask them about Lysias and his speeches and they would know a huge amount. Ask them about Solon, who lived 200 years earlier, and they were likely to look blank. OK, they had lectures which covered Solon and his democratic reforms, but (so far as I have observed) attending lectures conscientiously never quite hits the spot in the brain that writing an essay (*vel sim.*) does.

So I starting trying something rather different for their first piece of university work in ancient history. For a few years, I would ask them to go away and write me a history of the ancient world (eighth century BC to fifth century AD) in 1,500 words. This was great for a bit. They learned quite a lot, and produced mostly rather conservative stuff. But you could really open it up in the supervision – pointing out that half of them had not mentioned a single woman or slave, or that their view of 'the ancient world' had been entirely Graeco-Roman etc etc.

The trouble was that this assignment got to be part of the student mythology, so by the time the new first-years arrived in my room, the second-years had already tipped them off about what I was likely to ask. So this year I rang the changes, I gave them all a short essay to write on why the Old Oligarch (another set text) might be the best guide to fifth-century Athenian democracy that we have. (They had a decent bibliography and I gave them a 30-minute supervision, one to one, on what they each had written.) But for our communal class, all together, I set a rather different exercise.

I gave them two inscriptions from the Athenian fifth century, in Greek (and with a translation), and I asked them to come back prepared to say what these texts were and why they were interesting. I gave them no bibliography (though if they looked carefully at the introduction to the translation they would have seen a few hints). I said I didn't mind how they found out about them ... asking mates, Googling, discussing together, reference books ... but I wasn't going to help. The inscriptions, by the way, were the records of the Hermokopidae (the 'mutilators of the herms' and the 'profaners of the Eleusinian mysteries') auctioned after their trial (IG I/3, 426 and 30) and the Athenian regulations for the town of Chalcis, imposed after its attempted revolt from the Athenian empire (Meiggs/Lewis 52.)

To be honest, they looked a bit horrified when I explained this task. Most of them had never seen a Greek inscription before – didn't even know they existed, I guess. And, in fact, when I explained to my own old Director of Studies (Joyce Reynolds, now in her 90s) what I had set for the first-years, she said that she thought it was rather a 'stiff' exercise. (Frankly, I thought this was a bit rich. Back in the mid-1970s we had learned huge amounts from her by being given much more impossible tasks.)

Anyway, a week later they came to their joint supervision, brilliantly prepared to talk about these texts. They had got together, they had shared their knowledge, they had Googled and explored the library ... and they could really talk about what these utterly unfamiliar inscriptions had to say. And they had learned a little bit about what research was really like, and they hadn't just followed the bibliography (because they didn't have one!). I was delighted, and they were really launched I think.

So next year I shall do something similar – though I shall have to shake up the texts, otherwise these kids will just pass on their expertise to the new girls next year. 'Ah yes, we did that … what you need to say is … '

Anyone who wants to explore the task I set will find an English translation of these texts in Charles W. Fornara, Archaic Times to the End of the Peloponnesian War *(Cambridge UP, paperback, 1983).*

Comments

A 1,500 word history of the ancient world (eighth century BC to fifth century AD) with no mention of a woman or a slave or of what the Chinese were doing during those 1,300 years – tsk, tsk! And no mention of blacks or the disabled or, heaven help us! the gay and transgendered. Clearly those neophyte Classicists need their consciousness raised.
PL

Actually PL, it wasn't China that was uppermost in my mind … it was more the neighbours of 'Greece' and 'Rome' around the Mediterranean … Egypt, Lycia, Macedon.
MARY BEARD

Can I say without offence, Professor Beard, that you have, for me, just now entered Dante's Lower than Lowest Circle of Hell, which is populated by Those Who Set Wide-Ranging Essay Topics With A Minuscule Word Limit.

Low word-limits are appropriate for limited topics only.

ANNA

I'm tempted to suggest that 'Did the Trojan War Actually Happen?' could be satisfactorily answered in three words (plus a footnote or two, and bibliography, I suppose): 'Yes. So what?'

RICHARD

Did the Trojan War actually happen? Yes, it all started with an apple.

ANTHONY ALCOCK

Unde malum? A malo.

OLIVER NICHOLSON

de malo bonus est iocus hic quem scripsit Oliver
nam malus peperit mala tulitque mala.
Prose translation for the non-Latinists: 'This joke about the apple, that Oliver wrote, is a good one, for the apple tree produced apples and brought evils.'

[It's a pun on 'malum' = evil and 'malum' = apple]

MICHAEL BULLEY

Bold and malicious, a Golden Delicious.

ANTHONY ALCOCK

About essay-writing. When I was in year 3, I moaned to my Greek History tutor that I no longer knew what I was doing when I wrote an essay. He said, 'Mr Potts, if you can write an essay by the time you leave this place, we shall consider your education to have been a success.'

It occurs to me that Ludwig Wittgenstein never wrote an essay in his life. Why is it so important to be able to do so?

PAUL POTTS

Who gives a stuff about the Act of Settlement?

28 October 2011

I have to confess that I have always thought it was to the great good fortune of the female members of the royal family that they didn't have to face the awful prospect of the throne, unless they were unusually deficient in the brother department. Just occasionally discrimination can work, inadvertently, to our favour.

For me, it's rather like not being able to go to Mount Athos. Of course, I tend to protest publicly that it is 'men-only', but secretly I feel a twinge of relief that I don't have to go there, or have a view on the place, or join in those dreary conversations about old Father Demetrios … and so forth.

But since getting called twice by radio journalists in the last 24 hours to say something about changing the Act of Settlement etc., and about girls getting an equal chance to get to be monarch as men, I've found I have rather stronger views.

For a start, what *is* the point with tinkering with the monarchy – as if a tiny bit of political correctness could bring it up to date? You don't make a medieval/Victorian institution 'fair' by rearranging the deckchairs like this. The whole institution is unfair, like it or lump it. That I think was more or less Alexander Chancellor's view in the paper this morning. 'The daughters of monarchs are obviously as qualified (or unqualified) to succeed them as their sons, but the only way to deal with something as illogical as hereditary monarchy is to abolish it or accept it in all its weirdness.'

In fact, I suspect that in 200 years' time, we'll look back to this reform as the beginning of the end of the whole institution – as its much more serious inequities, its mad fantasies, get seen in even more clear relief, once this little bit of discrimination is removed.

But more to the point, fretting about the monarchy is almost always a political displacement activity.

Just reflect on the hours of parliamentary time that are going to go down this particular drain, when our MPs might actually be devoting their time and attention to banks, jobs, universities or whatever.

And just reflect on the effort and interest, across the Commonwealth, that will be devoted to the possibility that Kate and Wills's baby Princess might succeed to the throne, when there are millions of women in those territories who are still waiting for a proper education, or a proper job ... Priorities, priorities, priorities?

Anyway, when I ranted along these lines to the said journalists, I found that I didn't get invited to share these views with the listeners! Funny that.

Comments

Three cheers for Clovis.

The Swedes seem to have managed the transition, fairly painlessly, from agnatism to equal primogeniture a couple of decades ago.

ANTHONY ALCOCK

So a monarch's first-born will no longer be deprived of the throne because of the accident of her sex. Only the monarch's second-born will be deprived of the throne because of his or her accidental place in the birth order. And 99.9999999% of British citizens will be deprived of the throne because of the accident (not their fault) that neither of their parents happens to be the monarch. The idiocy of this is staggering.

PL

Quick, to Pseuds' Corner!

LUIS A NAVARRO

When you think of Royalty's habit of passing itself around, any of us with roots in Britain going back more than a generation or two are likely to be Royal Family without knowing it. I once saw a family tree on my mother's mother's side; it went back, partly on the legitimate and partly on the illegitimate side, to a bastard of Lionel of Antwerp, a younger son of Edward III. That presumably makes me 20-millionth or so in the line of succession. Some of you can doubtless do better.

TIM WEAKLEY

Better a dictator than a technocrat

16 November 2011

You can see the problem for Italy and Greece. But were Mario Monti and Lucas Papademos really the only feasible solutions? To go from the mad excesses of (what turned out to be) foolish democracy to the de facto imposition of an entirely unelected leader (approved, no doubt, by the Eurocrats) seems a bit of a 'frying-pan-into-the-fire' situation.

Sure, sensible political systems have some fall-back position for how to cope in a crisis, when the usual democratic arrangements are in danger of simply not managing. The Republican Romans had the institution of 'dictatorship', which on balance seems a better option than these technocrats (a term which is not far short of a euphemism for 'banker').

The trouble about 'dictator' is that the institution got nastily tainted in the first century BC by Lucius Cornelius Sulla and Julius Caesar – both of whom, in their different ways, hijacked the office for long-term, autocratic one-man rule, and radical political reform (ultimately to the benefit of themselves and/or their faction). That's the sense that 'dictatorship' still has.

But before that, it really was a short-term emergency office; certainly not sinister.

One of the basic principles of politics in Republican Rome was that political office was always shared. No one held political office independently, but always with a colleague. So even the very highest office, the consulship, was shared between two men. (This was largely an attempt to safeguard the political system against anyone making himself a king.) Sometimes, however, for the most part when the Romans were facing a particularly tough military opponent, there was a feeling that 'joint command' (for the consuls acted as military generals as well as civilian politicians) wasn't going to bring off victory, that one man was needed to make the big decisions on his own, not in committee. On those occasions a 'dictator' was nominated by the senate or consuls themselves. They were to serve for an absolute maximum of six months, and were supposed to lay down the office anyway once the crisis had passed.

One of the most famous of these dictators was Cincinnatus (whose name lies behind the city of Cincinnati). In our terms he was a right-wing ideologue, but he was a hero of propriety when it came to the dictatorship. Having been consul in the past, he accepted the senate's request that he become dictator while working on his farm ('Cincinnatus called from the plough', as his tag-line went), and as soon as he had secured the victory, he laid the office down. The famous modern sculpture shows him giving back the symbols of the dictatorship (the *fasces*) and returning to the plough.

The advantages of this over the technocrats? For a start, the time period for the suspension of democratic government was strictly limited. Secondly, this wasn't the flying in of someone outside the political process; dictators were generally senior figures who had previously been democratically elected to political office.

Pity the 'dictatorship' got abused and got a bad name. Come to think of it, maybe 'technocrat' will have become a term of abuse in a thousand years' time.

Comments

Technocracy in Greece? Wouldn't Plato have approved?

LV

Online etiquette

22 November 2011

One of the things that I really like about this blog is that the commenters are (by and large!) courteous, on-topic and full of relevant learning (and languages). The comments engage with, and add to, the blog. Most people have read the original post very carefully … too carefully sometimes, if you ask me (that's why they pick up all the errors of punctuation … but thanks anyway). And they (I mean, you) make the blog more than the sum of its parts.

I've only recently come to realise quite how different we are from the usual online postings. I've been doing a few BBC talks, and the comments on these are nothing of our sort. There are some careful engagements, that's true, and I'm hugely grateful for those, whether pro or anti. But a frightening lot of the comments that appear on the Have Your Say BBC website seem to be driven by different versions of bile. Same is true for the *Guardian* Comment, and at least one thread on Mumsnet (though not all) … or really any big commenting site.

There is an awful lot of 'this is rubbish', 'you are a complete idiot to write this' … or 'ho ho old lady, do you have a beard?'

My first reaction is slight fear. My second is to wonder what makes otherwise ordinary people write this vicious stuff when they get on-line, when they wouldn't do so otherwise. It is partly the pseudonyms, I think. On this blog most commenters use their own names, or their first names or initials: you/we/I are there as 'us'. On an awful lot of big public blogs people adopt all kinds of *noms de comment* … like 'StrawberryJam' or 'RainingCatsandDogs' or 'QueenElizabeth1' and so on. My hunch is that this kind of 'para-identity' somehow allows people to write in a way that they would never do under their own names. It gives them a licence to be rude, in a way that they would never be face-to-face.

Strangely (and a bit unnervingly), some keen commenters seem to bond with their sobriquets. When I misremembered the complicated sobriquet of one regular commenter on the Mumsnet thread, she replied that it was an insult to get it wrong. An insult not to remember an on-line nickname? Come on …

I also have the sense – when people are commenting on my on-line articles – that *they* think they are talking on-line about someone who isn't really a person. That's partly why I respond to some of even the most aggressive comments. It's just to remind everyone that there is 'me', a real person, there. And actually one who might be hurt by unmitigated vitriol.

I also think that *never* to reply is bad in itself. If you 'put yourself about' on the web or the radio, there is a duty (and in a way a pleasure) to respond and discuss. It not only reminds the commenter that there is a human being involved; it also confirms the general idea that we're in dialogue, not just in lecture. And I have found some good friends this way, in the constructive disagreements between author and reader you can set up with new technology.

All the same, I do have one basic rule for on-line commenting. Cut all that 'rubbish' and 'idiot' talk; only respond on the web as you would do if you were talking face-to-face. For me, it's a bit like reviewing: only say what you would say if you met the reviewee over a drink.

Comments

I would take issue with your frankly rather snide comments about pseudonymity. I've had a pseudonymous identity on the internet for almost ten years now – yes, the same, continuous identity. This is not because I'm running around bashing people on-line, but because I would much prefer that my on-line hobbies – though innocuous – not be fully accessible to all and sundry, particularly future employers, via a Google search.

SIRIANNE

Well said, though I do think that there's a great deal more bile out there than you imagine. The sites you mention – Mumsnet, the *Guardian* and the BBC – are models of decorum compared to some.

However, I don't think that the use of pseudonyms is much of a contributing factor. Here I agree with Sirianne. My own pseudonym came about simply because originally I used to post only on matters connected to my own profession and industry, and occasionally I expressed views which differed from the public and corporate positions taken by my employers, even though privately they might have agreed. The only solution to this conundrum was to use a pseudonym, or not to post anything which might displease my present employers or prospective future ones. Then I discovered that I had built a history, a reputation (I only ever use this pseudonym) and an online community of like-minded people that I'm now reluctant to abandon.

CHURM RINCEWIND

I wonder what Sirianne's innocuous online hobbies are, that she doesn't want 'all and sundry, particularly future employers' to learn about.

TIM WEAKLEY

Knitting and crocheting, mostly! Together with discussion of (objectively not so good, I admit) SF and fantasy TV shows in probably more detail than the average member of a university hiring committee would be comfortable with. Nothing that would shock my aged gran, I assure you.

SIRIANNE

The phenomenon you refer to is the on-line disinhibition effect, known colloquially (including in academic circles outside trade journals) as GIFT: the Greater Internet Fuckwad Theory. The equation is: normal person + anonymity + audience = total fuckwad. It has been proven time and time again by such comments as you have yourself received.

And on a fascinating Classical note, the idea apparently was originally proposed by Plato in his story about the Ring of Gyges.

CERBERUS

There was the recent case of a woman who sued for divorce (in the real world) because her husband's internet character in some on-line game had been unfaithful to her own character with some other real woman's character in the same game. I'm not saying the people who comment on Mary Beard's blog under a pseudonym would go that far, but I think you can see the beginnings of the slippery slope.

MICHAEL BULLEY

I hate to say it, but your online etiquette piece sounded like
a schoolteacher's rules for engagement – listen and behave
yourselves, otherwise I won't reply. Blogging is the opportunity for
adults and young at heart to express themselves in a way which
makes them feel most comfortable, sobriquets notwithstanding,
and in this diverse world of ours I would like to think that we could
cope with others' warts as well as their smiles. For somebody billed
as 'wickedly subversive' it would be in keeping with this image to
poke fun in return. Sometimes, your more acerbic responses are
hilarious, rudeness aside.

A DENNIS

Educational tourism

30 November 2011

There is something deeply frustrating about many of the bright new educational ideas headlined by all political parties. I mean the 'educational tourism' ones. They are easy to recognise. Some minister or shadow minister has been on a visit to Norway, the United States or wherever, and returns home with an 'idea' for schools or universities – whether it is how to raise the basic skills of 11-year-olds, or how to increase diversity among undergraduates – which they proceed to wave around (often accusing the educational professionals here of blindness to exciting new developments overseas).

They sometimes haven't got wise even to such problems of these schemes as could be discovered by a quick trawl on Google (the issues surrounding New York charter schools, for example). They sometimes don't appear to have thought about the key structural differences between one (superficially similar) system and another.

That is especially apparent in admissions to university, where the USA and the UK are really non-comparable – for the simple reason that American kids normally aren't entering into subject-specific degree programmes right away, but specialise later. So they can reasonably be selected by non-specialists (who might indeed be charged with particular targets for ethnicity, social background etc.). We, on the other hand, are normally choosing students for specialised courses, to be completed in three years. You surely have to involve specialists, not general administrators, for that.

For universities, America is the usual stick with which the
UK higher education sector is beaten. Some US universities
are truly, truly excellent (albeit different from what we expect).
But not all. So it was useful to read Tony Grafton's article in the
New York Review of Books last week (24 November), discussing
American universities across the board. Take the time an
undergraduate student spends to get a degree at even the best
public institutions: in a handful, 90% or more graduate within
six years; most have a much lower rate than that … and the
drop-out rate (not simply delayed completion) is much higher
than anything we would be happy to accept. This article should
be required reading for every minister of higher education.

The funny thing is that I saw the 'boot on the other foot'
a few days ago, and had a glimpse of what happens when you
talk about the UK system when you don't really understand
it. I was reading Martha Nussbaum's new book *Not for Profit*
– in all sorts of ways, an excellent defence of the humanities
at university level. But when she gets on to the terrible things
that are happening in British universities, she is seriously
misleading. True, terrible things are happening, but not quite
what she implies.

'British faculty do not have tenure any longer, so there is
no barrier to firing them at any time', she writes. True, 'tenure'
was abolished, with the result that academics can now be made
redundant (and departments closed); and I am sure that has
sometimes been misused. But that is not to say that they can
be fired at any time (and of course they could have been fired
before, when they had 'tenure' for a variety of crimes, like
'gross moral turpitude' or whatever).

And she goes on to suggest that there is no regular
sabbatical system in the UK any longer and the only way that

we can get leave is by applying for competitive grants. Again, simply not true in that form.

You have to be careful when you stray into some other country's educational system.

Comments

Ah yes, the wonderful charge of gross moral turpitude. JBS Haldane was accused of that, although the term may have been 'gross immorality'. He had deliberately got caught in bed with the lady he was to marry, in order to secure her a divorce. He appealed successfully against the charge, I think on the basis that while it was moral turpitude (or immorality, as the case may have been), it was not gross.

RICHARD BARON

One of the major reasons that five to six years is the 'average' time needed to complete a university degree in the United States is because the classes that a student must take (we call them 'required courses') in order to graduate are often oversubscribed. It is not unusual for a student to have to wait several years before there is room for him/her in a required class. So, it is not a problem of a student's limited ability, but rather a problem of overcrowding.

EILEEN

In my experience as head of a teachers' union in Australia for some years, top bureaucrats read the journals, listen to the gurus and go on 'study trips', then come back and sell their newly acquired, recycled, 'initiatives' to their minister, who, knowing little about education except their own, falls for it and believes it will get him/her seen as the country's brightest star.

It is then pushed down on to powerless teachers, who recognise immediately the unlikeliness of it to do anything to improve education but can do nothing to prevent it till the next new idea, which is usually equally bad. And so we progress ...

JEAN

Cor blimey! I was gobstruck when I read Eileen's letter so I checked some of the facts.

It does seem to be true that only 57% of American college students complete a four-year degree course within six years.

This in itself is extraordinary, but it was not really what amazed and shocked me. It seems that colleges do not provide facilities for all students to attend required classes, so students have to wait several years before a place becomes available on one of these courses.

Colleges admit students to courses and don't provide the facilities for them to complete the course.

TOHU

Juliet's balcony

Tourist hot-spots come in many different guises. Only a couple of weeks ago the queue to get into the Colosseum was about an hour and a half in length – and all to see the rather depressing ruins inside the building, which are nothing compared with the splendid outside. (Tip: if you really want to see the Colosseum, go to one of the entrances to the Forum and buy the ticket there ... the queue is never so long.)

In Verona, where we finished our stint of filming yesterday (not the amphitheatre, in case you are wondering), the place to go is the 'House of Juliet', complete with balcony, as in *Romeo and Juliet*. There were no actual queues, but a tremendous, polyglot crush, even in mid-December – made all the more democratic by the fact that the view of the balcony and other bric-à-brac is free. You only have to pay if you want actually to go and stand on it, and to see the other Juliet memorabilia in the 'museum' ... pride of place going to the bed that starred in Zeffirelli's version of Shakespeare's play.

Of course, the place has nothing to do with the non-existent Juliet at all, and was a clever invention of the nineteenth century, turned into a veritable tourist attraction in the 1930s. But overall it is as odd as the Colosseum, with the added tinge of slightly off-putting, slightly leering, slightly touching 'romance'.

One high spot of the museum itself for most people is the opportunity to send an email (or even an old-style letter) to Juliet, who – it seems – will answer you (unless you are too

filthy in what you choose to say to her). Indeed it appears that
they have a whole team of people employed just to answer the
emails that Juliet receives in the 'Club Juliet'.

But if you can't afford the 6 euros to go inside, there is still
plenty to do. The walls of the entrance-way to Juliet's House
are covered with the graffiti of at least the last few years of
hopeless romantics – as if scrawling your name in the vicinity
of a mythical balcony of a mythical couple somehow gives it
added force.

But the weirdest thing was the 1970s' bronze statue of
Juliet standing just underneath the balcony. It was clear
from the 'polish', and by watching what people actually did,
that one hallowed custom was to go up and grasp Juliet's
right breast, and have your photo taken in the act. This was
the sport of almost every visitor from the seven-year-olds
to the 70-somethings, male and female. A few looked a bit
embarrassed. Most entered into the spirit of the fondle.

A new ritual, a bit tacky – but bringing the star-crossed lovers down to size.

Comments

Grasping the breast? Maybe a fertility rite or a good-luck wish? One wonders what Frazer would have made of it.

ANNA

I'm surprised, bearing in mind today's social climate, that the fondlers have not been placed on a lifetime police register as sexual predators. Epstein's stone Assyrian thingummy carved on Oscar Wilde's gravestone in Père Lachaise cemetery used to have a large and distinctive penis that was polished by many hands touching it … it was broken off many years ago.

LORD TRUTH/RONALD ROGERS

From *New York Times* (15 December): 'Recently, descendants of Wilde, the Irish dramatist and wit who died here in 1900, decided to have his immense gravestone cleansed of a vast accumulation of lipstick markings from kisses left by admirers, who for years have been defacing, and some say eroding, the memorial in hilly Père Lachaise Cemetery here. But the decision meant not only cleaning the stone, a flying nude angel by the sculptor Jacob Epstein, who was inspired by the British Museum's Assyrian figures, but also erecting a seven-foot plate glass wall to keep ardent admirers at a distance.'

NICK JOWETT

Christmas tradition – and innovation

25 December 2011

'Tradition always incorporates innovation' insisted the daughter (an anthropologist-cum-historian) on Christmas Eve. The reason for her insistence on this great anthropological truth was her desire that this year we should try roasting rather than boiling the sprouts for Christmas dinner.

Predictably enough, we chose to follow that other anthropological model: namely, 'accretion'. The husband had liked our encounter with roast sprouts in the USA but rather doubted our ability to do them well enough on our first try (and anyway, he is still quite partial to boiled ones). So – as we had laid in well more sprouts than we needed – we decided to roast half and boil half, just to be on the safe side. (I expect that we will now do this sprouting double act as long as we have Christmas together.)

At this point, I rather pretentiously observed that our decision followed the model of our Christmas tree ... it was growing tradition, a bit like the way we put new decorations on the tree each year, without throwing away the old ones. To be precise: a rather jolly hart, vaguely taken from the Wilton Diptych, joined the line-up this year, as did a shining ship (supposedly based on Turner's *Fighting Temeraire*).

Conversation, let me reassure you, doesn't usually run along these lines over our kitchen table. But it was perhaps a nice reminder of what a wonderful anthropological case-study modern Christmas can be. In fact a friend of mine, Sue Benson, who taught Anthropology in Cambridge, often used to ask candidates at their interviews to comment anthropologically on Christmas. She was never very impressed by those who went on about the terrible 'commercialism' of it all; she was looking for a bit of analysis of our nostalgia, and the way the celebration (for many, no matter what religion – if any) still acts as a re-affirmation of ties of friendship, a focus of remembrance, not to mention gift exchange.

Sadly, for me, it now acts as a focus of remembrance of her. She died a few years ago, but Sue's question to her candidates (as well as her whole-hearted, exuberantly atheistic investment in all the festivities of the season) is now always part of what I think when I 'think Christmas'. Exactly, she would have said. For that's the way that Christmas comes to mean more, the older you get ... generating and preserving an ever increasing number of things to remember. (And I'm sure that's how she used to press her interview candidates.)

But Christmas isn't just a great case study for the anthropologically inclined. Classicists get a toe-hold in there too.

That's because, somewhere lurking behind our celebrations (though, in truth, the connections are a bit hard to follow) is the Roman festival of Saturnalia – eventually a seven-day holiday at the end of December; just like our Christmas break, it got longer as time went on. There's nothing a Classicist likes doing better at this time of year than sounding off about the similarities and differences between our festivities and the Romans'.

The basic point is that the Saturnalia wasn't really a match for the over-consumption of Christmas dinner. That has a Roman feel in its own way (and I bet the Romans would have loved the ritual of lighting the brandy over the Christmas pud, if only they had invented matches). But much more similar are the rituals of gift-giving, games and silly hats. And even more distinctive is the idea of role reversal. For once a year, on the Saturnalia, Roman slaves are said to have sat down to dinner, served by their masters. (No one is very explicit about who actually cooked it, but I suspect the slaves …)

It was in other words, almost the spitting image of the classic 'office party', in which the Managing Director makes a gracious display of serving the wine, while trying desperately and unsuccessfully to remember the names of all the lowly staff (thus rather ruining the point of the occasion). Presumably the same problems emerged in ancient Rome, with the toffs repeatedly mixing up their poor Lurcios and their Pseudoluses.

Not sure if it counts as one of the better Roman inventions.

Happy Christmas everyone!

Comments

Heinrich Böll, in 1947, wrote a short novel called *Und nicht nur zur Weihnachtszeit* ('And Not Only at Christmas'). The basic story is that an elderly woman, unable to celebrate Christmas from 1940 to the end of the war, makes up for it big-time after the war by having her family celebrate it every day (a form of of 'Christmas tree therapy' for her), until members of her family, unable to stand it any longer, stop attending the festivities and eventually scarper, having themselves replaced by actors. One of them, a professional boxer, ends up as a lay brother in a monastery.

ANTHONY ALCOCK

I was once asked by a very American person, 'And what do you do for Christmas, Paul?' I said, 'I buy a bottle of whiskey, go to bed, and come out when it's all over.' He was profoundly shocked.

PAUL POTTS

Five thoughts on getting to 57

31 December 2011

I am in a couple of hours 57 years old. My rather elderly (aged 40) mother gave birth, old-style, in Much Wenlock Cottage Hospital on 1 January 1955 ... with a midwife and the local GP, who (as he and Mum always used to joke, for years after) only got there when everything was more or less over. (This isn't just self-obsession – it's a story I heard repeated at the said GP's Xmas party for years and years in my childhood and adolescence ... with greater or lesser shades of embarrassment, on my part.)

So my birthday has always been (for me) a New Year occasion. And always bound up with New Year's Eve ... everybody is pissed and enjoying the 'rite of passage', and at some point after midnight I nerve myself to say (or not to say) 'and ... errr ... excuse me ... it's my birthday.'

Anyway, at 57, happily and very very gratefully married for more than a quarter of a century ... five thoughts on birthdays as you get old(er).

1) **Bloody lucky (version 1).** I am still alive, 57 years on. I've survived two children and various bits of medical intervention (including a benign breast lump/aka clot of milk, when I was breast-feeding, and that seemed like imminent death at the time). Most of the people I work on (the Romans) were dead or dying by their late 50s. So thank the Lord, and modern medicine.

2) **Bloody lucky (version 2).** By immense good fortune, things have gone really well for me in the last few years, and I've done stuff that my Mum and Dad would never have dreamed of, though would have loved. Some of the little triumphs seem a bit silly. But I am really chuffed that I've been on *Desert Island Discs*, and *Any Questions*; and I've written books that colleagues have liked, as well as the 'general public' … I even got a book prize. And I now get offered more books to review, or radio programmes to make, than I could ever do. (OK, in the great order of things, not a key indicator … not a big deal maybe, but when I think back 20 years, I would have felt it a huge success when anyone asked me to do anything like that.)

And let me say to any young female academic with a brood of kids, who thinks her career is going down the tubes … so was mine (as several of my more waspish male colleagues enjoyed saying) back then, a couple of decades ago … I hadn't written enough stuff; I had too few outcomes; and in fact people talked about the 'tragedy' of my career. But stick in there, keep your name on the map and don't let the buggers get you down. Don't, don't give up. And accept that offer to review a book …

3) **Anxious.** Well anyone my age is anxious about what happens next. One of my best mates said to me when he turned 60 that the bad thing was that, after 60, any illness might be your last. And indeed it was almost true for him. He died almost a decade ago. So, let's face it, each visit to the doctor is more loaded now.

But I'm also anxious about 'the media'. So far, with only a very few exceptions, they have been very kind to me. I have blathered on about the ancient world, and worse, and the critics haven't said 'Oh for f***'s sake, shut up.' But who knows what next? (I am just making a mini-series for BBC 2 that I hope you all like; but I'm on tenterhooks, honestly.)

4) **Memories.** When I was a little kid and asked what happened when you died, my Mum always came out with the old cliché about 'living in people's memories'. It wasn't nearly good enough at the time, but I begin to see what she meant. For me, as for most of us I imagine, memory is a bigger and bigger thing, even in the fleeting, just-a-nod-to-it, sense. And that includes all kinds of stuff from schoolroom trauma to long-past, ancient passions – in a way I would never have expected.

I still vividly recall all those unlikely and memorable sites of serious adolescent love with unserious (or wholly unsuitable) partners ... from Hawkestone Park to Rose Cottage, Ironbridge, or the in-your-face rhododendrons at Attingham. Every day I find those guys, and those places, come through my head – as my dead parents do, usually in a nicely teasing way. (I guess it never stops ... years ago I reviewed a biography of Naomi Mitchison, and I called attention, with a degree of disbelief, to the moment when she made love to Wade-Gery in a snow storm outside Oxford; she sent me a card, aged 80-something, to say that it really was snowing that day.)

5) **Humility.** Obvious really ... but when things are going well, just remember how different it might be, how easily.

And this, I guess, is the time to say that we plan another 'don's life' book picking up where the last left off. Hope you'll all be on board. As I've said before, the commenters make this blog. Thanks everyone, and good luck for next year.

Comments

It is not just the ever-increasing stock of personal memories that is a pleasure. As one ages (I am three years behind you), the proportion of the population who can remember more world events than oneself diminishes. This creates at least the illusion of relative wisdom, and possibly the reality. In our youth, the majority of the population had at least some memory of the Second World War, even if only childhood or teenage memories, and there was a sense of a gap in one's own experience. Now the majority don't even remember the Moon landings. The youngsters are the ones with the gap.

On the scary side, we must face the fact that people younger than ourselves now have their fingers on the nuclear button. At least Angela Merkel, whose finger is on the Euro button, is older.

RICHARD BARON

I can still vaguely remember when you came into the library of the British School at Rome, insisting that Derrida's book *On Grammatology* was a work without which no self-respecting academic library could do. The poor librarian had no idea what you were talking about.

The road from meaningless intellectual gibberish to *Desert Island Discs* has probably been hard, but worth it.

ANTHONY ALCOCK

I never read *On Grammatology* properly when I should have done, but I still have a copy, and my next project is to go back to it. One effect of that nonsense (or gibberish) is that it makes readers realise how little they understand what they thought they thought.

PAUL POTTS

Afterword

Times change.

Only three years ago I ended my first book of blogs (*It's a Dons Life*) with a serious few pages justifying the whole practice of blogging. It was not, I wanted to assure readers (and no doubt myself too), a cheap, dumbed-down form of journalism; the hyper-links could open up a whole range of learned information that could never be included in a traditional print article; and the instant international reach of the web made blogs an important new medium of political comment and protest. (Don't forget that in 2009 the TimesOnline site was still calling its blogs, 'web-logs'.)

Three years on, that all sounds needlessly defensive, if not quaintly old-fashioned. Who could possibly question the seriousness of a blog of 600+ words, not to mention the links, when the world is now full of 140-character tweets. As you will have spotted (p. 165), after a bit of heart-searching I now have a Twitter account, but then so do such august institutions as the British Academy and the British Museum. And, in fact, we're told that the 'Arab Spring' was launched by Twitter and Facebook. I'm never quite sure if I believe it, but if it's even half-true, it takes 'the new medium of political comment' to a rather different level.

I also stopped to reflect, back then, on the edgy relationship between print and on-line reading. Turning my blogs into a proper book, I suggested, was to provide a different reading experience (browsing and flipping) and to give them a life beyond the screen:

> No one I know reads their laptop on the Underground, in bed or in the loo. So here we have *A Don's Life* for the journey to work, for going to sleep – or for the smallest room in the house.

That too now seems a bit quaint – as all of you reading these words on your Kindle screen in the loo will be able to confirm.

But in those last few years the relations between print and on-line news media have changed even more radically than that. I don't just mean that print journalists now often find their stories from trawling the blogs (as happened to my little squib about the college grace, p. 32, and left me with a bit of explaining to do with the colleagues). But some newspapers are actually busy turning themselves into what is in effect a 'mega-blog', with the print paper as just an optional extra.

I have become more laid-back, less worried, about all this. Personally, I'm a great fan of the traditional book, and I hope that many of you are reading this between soft paper covers. But what really matters is not the medium of the writing – but whether the writer has got anything to say.

I am still not entirely convinced that many tweets *do* have anything to say; I hope these blogs pass the test better.

Acknowledgements

A blog is a communal enterprise, so my first thanks go to all those who read and comment on 'A Don's Life' and especially to those who have allowed their comments to be reprinted here. You may not know it, but I get up in the morning and go to the blog ... wondering what you have had to say.

Then my thanks go to all at the *TLS* and *TimesOnline* who first thought of the idea and have hosted 'A Don's Life' ever since: especially now Michael Caines, Lucy Dallas, and Peter Stothard (who was the blog's *fons et origo*). My family has been patient of my blogging habits; they have suggested topics and allowed themselves to be discussed. So thanks to Robin Cormack ('the husband'), to Zoe ('the daughter') and Raphael ('the son'). My colleagues in Cambridge have been similarly tolerant, even when it has been inconvenient. Thank you, Newnham and the Classics Faculty.

At Profile, this book was again the brainchild of Peter Carson (who vetoed any moaning posts about the train from Cambridge to London, you will be relieved to know). And I am grateful too for all the support of Penny Daniel, Andrew Franklin, Ruth Killick, Matthew Taylor and Valentina Zanca.

Last, but emphatically not least, Debbie Whittaker in Cambridge has helped with the selection of posts and comments, the permissions, and almost every aspect of the conversion of the blog into a book.

So, thank you one and all.

Picture Credits